PALL MALL
BIBLIOGRAPHIES
No. 3
FOUR METAPHYSICAL POETS

PALL MALL BIBLIOGRAPHIES

A Series of bibliographical catalogues of the early editions of the works of important authors

This series aims to provide, in a form suitable for quick and easy reference, accurate bibliographical details of the early appearance in print of the works of important writers. In planning it, the publishers have had in mind the needs both of the scholar working on the transmission of a text and of the librarian, collector or bookseller who wants to identify quickly a particular edition or issue. A special feature of the series is that every bibliographical description will be accompanied by a photographic facsimile of the title-page of the book.

Each catalogue will describe all the editions, issues and major variants of an author's works published during his lifetime and for a short period after his death. The length of this period will vary in different cases, the aim being to include every publication falling within the terms of reference and in which the author himself, his literary executors or others who had known him may have had a hand. The terms of reference cover collections of the author's writings, single original works, translations from other writers, works written in collaboration, anthologies in which the author's contributions formed the major part, doubtful and even spurious compositions if there was strong contemporary belief in their authenticity.

Each volume will comprise the following main features:

1. A short introduction on the author's life and publications, with a chronological table and references to any important bibliographical studies which have been published about him.
2. Descriptions of all editions, issues and major variants of his works published during the period defined. The main classification will be by titles, arranged in alphabetical order; there will be cross-references from alternative titles. Under each title-heading entries will be in chronological order. Every entry will contain: (a) Short-title, imprint and date, followed by a reference to the plate number of the titlepage facsimile; (b) Collation; (c) List of contents; (d) Note of copies seen; (e) Bibliographical references.
3. Photographic facsimiles of titlepages, keyed to the entries in (2).
4. Indexes of editors, collaborators, translators, printers and publishers.

FOUR
METAPHYSICAL
POETS

GEORGE HERBERT   RICHARD CRASHAW
HENRY VAUGHAN   ANDREW MARVELL

*A Bibliographical Catalogue of the Early Editions
of their Poetry and Prose*

(*To the end of the 17th century*)

by

A. F. ALLISON

1973
DAWSONS OF PALL MALL
Folkestone & London

Published by
DAWSONS OF PALL MALL
Cannon House
Folkestone, Kent, England

ISBN: 0 7129 0599 5

© Wm. Dawson & Son Ltd., 1973

c e

Printed in Great Britain
by Photolithography
Unwin Brothers Limited
Old Woking, Surrey

CONTENTS

5

FOREWORD

The four writers whose works form the subject of this catalogue need no general biographical introduction. Brief notes of the main events of each writer's life have, however, been included at the beginning of the section devoted to his works in order to provide the necessary background to the chronological list of publications.

The catalogue follows the general plan of the previous publications in this series. For the bibliographical descriptions I have taken as a general guide Greg's *Bibliography of the Printed Drama to the Restoration* but I have simplified Greg's formulae a little and introduced one or two other changes, my aim being to give rather less detail than Greg does and to concentrate on points that will enable the user to identify easily the edition or issue of a book that he has in his hands even though the copy may be imperfect. The following points call for mention: (1) Since the title page of every item is reproduced in photographic facsimile, only a conventional short-title appears at the head of the bibliographical descriptions. (2) In the lists of contents I have not followed Greg's practice of putting the signature reference after the item listed; thus, I say: 'B1 text', and not 'Text B1'. (3) In addition to mentioning head-titles (abbreviated to HT) and ornamental initials when they occur on the first page of text, I state the kind of ornament (if any) to be found at the head of this page, e.g. headpiece (abbreviated to HP), lace ornament, band of printer's type-ornament. (4) the abbreviation 'Anon.' indicates that the author's name is not revealed in the book. (5) The identification of printers, where their names do not appear in the book, is given in the form: 'Printer: Thomas Roycroft'. This is shorthand for Greg's 'The printer appears from his ornaments and initials to be. . .'. (6) Locations cited are of copies which I have myself examined or which have been looked at for me. No attempt has been made to provide a census of copies but the STC or Wing reference is followed by a plus sign if more copies are listed there. This is a departure from previous practice. Wing references are to the second edition for volume 1 (the only volume so far published in this edition) and to the first edition for volumes 2 and 3. (7) Pressmarks are given for all British Museum and Bodleian Library copies.

Works cited in Abbreviated Form in this Catalogue

Grosart.   The Complete Works . . . of Andrew Marvell . . . Edited, with memorial introductions and notes, by . . . A. B. Grosart. 4 vol. *London*, [1872–5].

Hutchinson.   The Works of George Herbert. Edited with a commentary by F. E. Hutchinson. *Oxford, Clarendon Press*, 1953.

Legouis.   Pierre Legouis, André Marvell, poète puritain, patriote, 1621–1678. [With a bibliography.] *Paris, Henri Didier; London, Oxford University Press*, 1928.

Andrew Marvell. Poet, Puritan, Patriot. *Oxford, Clarendon Press*, 1965. Second edition, 1968. The English editions are without the bibliography.

Margoliouth.   The Poems and Letters of Andrew Marvell. Edited by H. M. Margoliouth. Second edition. *Oxford, Clarendon Press*, 1952. Third edition . . . Revised by Pierre Legouis with the collaboration of E. E. Duncan-Jones, 1971.

Martin.   The Poems English Latin and Greek of Richard Crashaw. Edited by L. C. Martin. Second edition. *Oxford, Clarendon Press*, 1957.

The Works of Henry Vaughan. Edited by L. C. Martin. Second edition. *Oxford, Clarendon Press*, 1957.

SR   Stationers' Register, ed. Arber. *London*, 1875–94.

STC   A. W. Pollard and G. R. Redgrave, A Short-title Catalogue of Books printed in England, Scotland, & Ireland . . . 1475–1640. *London, Bibliographical Society*, 1926.

Wing   Donald Wing, A Short-title Catalogue of Books printed in England, Scotland, & Ireland . . . 1641–1700. 3 vol. *New York, Index Society*, 1945–51. Second edition of vol. 1, 1972.

Libraries and Collections cited in Abbreviated Form in this Catalogue

BM   British Museum, London.
Bodl. Bodleian Library, Oxford.
Dyce. Dyce Collection at the Victoria and Albert Museum, London.
Hunt. Henry E. Huntington Library, San Marino, California.
TCD. Trinity College, Dublin.
ULC. University Library, Cambridge.

HERBERT

HERBERT, George (1593–1633)

Son of Sir Richard Herbert and younger brother of Lord Herbert of Cherbury. Educated at Cambridge where he took his degree in 1616 and was Public Orator 1619–27. He won the favour of James I and was for a short time at court. Coming under the influence of Nicholas Ferrar of the Little Gidding community he rejected the worldly life and took orders in the Anglican church. In 1630 he became rector of Bemerton, Wiltshire, where he died three years later.

Chronology of the Publication of Herbert's Works to 1700

1623.   *Oratio qua Auspicatissimum Serenissimi Principis Caroli Reditum ex Hispaniis celebravit.* A speech made in his capacity as Public Orator of the university. Printed at Cambridge.

1633.   First and second editions of *The Temple*, a sequence of religious poems, edited after Herbert's death by Nicholas Ferrar. Printed at Cambridge.

1634.   Third edition of *The Temple*. Printed at Cambridge.

1635.   Fourth edition of *The Temple*. Printed at Cambridge.

1638.   Fifth edition of *The Temple*. Printed at Cambridge.

1640.   *Outlandish Proverbs.* A collection of proverbs from various sources, English and foreign. Printed at London.

1641.   Sixth edition of *The Temple*. Printed at Cambridge.

[c.1647] Seventh edition of *The Temple*. A pirated edition, printed probably at London.

1651.   Reissue of *Outlandish Proverbs* under the title *Jacula Prudentum* Published at London.

1652.   *Herbert's Remains.* Comprising the first edition of *A Priest to the Temple*, a prose work on the life and duties of a country parson, and a second, enlarged edition of *Outlandish Proverbs* under the title *Jacula Prudentum.* Edited by Barnabas Oley. Printed at London.

1656.   'Seventh' edition of *The Temple*. Printed at London.

1660.   Eighth edition of *The Temple*. Printed at London.

1667.   Ninth edition of *The Temple*. Printed at London.

1671.   Second edition of *A Priest to the Temple*, with Walton's Life of Herbert. Printed at London.

1674.   Tenth edition of *The Temple*, with Walton's Life. Printed at London.

1675.   Third edition of *A Priest to the Temple*, with Walton's Life. Printed at London.

1678. Eleventh edition of *The Temple*, with Walton's Life. Printed at London.

1695. 'Eleventh' edition of *The Temple*, with Walton's Life. A reissue of the tenth edition with the preliminaries reprinted. Published at London.

Herbert's Remains

See no. 6.

Jacula Prudentum

See nos. 3, 6.

Musae Responsoriae

Wing (H.1510) cites this as if it had been published separately in 1662; in fact, it forms part of a collection: 'Ecclesiastes Solomonis', by Joannes Vivianus, published in that year (Wing V.669). Not included in the present catalogue.

Oratio qua Auspicatissimum Serenissimi Principis Caroli Reditum ex Hispaniis celebravit

A speech in Latin delivered by Herbert as Public Orator of the University of Cambridge to celebrate the return of Prince Charles from Spain in October 1623. (Hutchinson pp. 444 et seq., 601 et seq.) No entry in SR.

[**1**] Oratio quâ auspicatissimum serenissimi principis Caroli reditum ex Hispaniis celebravit. [*Cambridge,*] *Ex Officina Cantrelli Legge,* 1623.

[**Plate 1**]

4⁰.¶⁴ 2¶⁴ (2¶4 blank).   Paginated (¶2) 1–11.

¶1 title (verso blank). ¶2 text beginning 'Veneranda Capita . . .', lace ornament and initial. 2¶3ᵛ blank.

Catchwords: ¶–2¶, sed   2¶2–3, Quam- [Quamobrem]

RT ORATIO.

BM (11764.cc.20) + 2¶4. Bodl. (Antiq.e. E 1623.6) + 2¶4; (Vet. A2e.231/2) + 2¶4; (Vet. A2 e.148/2)–2¶4. ULC.

STC 13181 (+)

Outlandish Proverbs

A collection of proberbs, many of them translated from foreign sources. The first edition of which any copies are known to survive, published in 1640, seven years after Herbert's death, is anonymous but has the words 'selected by Mr G. H.' on the titlepage; in the edition of 1651, Herbert is taken to be the author. The identification of 'G.H.' with George Herbert has sometimes been questioned but is now generally accepted (see Hutchinson, pp. 568 et seq.). 'Outlandish Proberbs' was entered separately in SR, on 24 September 1639, to Mathew Simmons, but no edition with Simmons's name is known: the extant 1640 edition has the imprint of Humphrey Blunden. 'Witts Recreations', with which some copies of this edition were issued (see note to no. 2 below), was entered in SR to Humphrey Blunden on 15 October 1639.

[2] Outlandish proverbs, selected by Mr G. H. *T.P. for Humphrey Blunden, 1640.* [**Plate 2**]

Anon. Printer: Thomas Paine. Of this edition some of the copies were probably issued separately, but at least some were bound up and issued with the first edition of *Witts Recreations*, 1640 (STC 25870), an anonymous compilation sometimes attributed to Sir John Mennes.

8⁰. A–D⁸ E⁴ (misprinting E2 as D2. E4 blank). Leaves unnumbered.

A1 title (verso blank). A2 text, with HT, HP and initial. E3ᵛ blank.

Catchwords: A–B, 212. The B–C, 439. He [439. Hee] D–E, 946. The RT *Outlandish Proverbs*.

Text ends at foot of E3 with proverb no. 1032 'Hee that wipes the childs nose . . .' and the word 'Finis'.

BM (G. 10382)–E4 (separate); (C.65.c.6)–E4 (with *Witts Recreations*). (In this copy E3 has been replaced by a leaf with proverbs nos. 1003–10 in a different setting of type. The text ends on E3ʳ with proverb no. 1010 'Without danger, we cannot get before [*sic* for 'beyond'] danger', followed by 'Finis', a rule and 'Imprimatur. 1639. Matth. Clay'. Hutchinson describes this leaf as a cancel. It seems more probable, however, that it witnesses to an earlier rather than a later state of the text. It is possibly a skilful type-facsimile, made at a later date from an early edition now lost, and inserted into this copy of the 1640 edition because the last leaf of text was missing.) Bodl. (8⁰ A 143 Art.) + E4 (with *Witts Recreations*).
STC 13182 and 25870 (+)

[3] [A reissue with a cancel title.] Jacula prudentum. Or, outlandish proverbs, sentences, &c. *T.M. for T. Garthwait, 1651.* [**Plate 3**]

Printer of the cancel title: Thomas Maxey.

Bodl. (Mal. 895)

Not in Wing.

[Another edition, enlarged.] Jacula prudentum. Or outlandish proverbs. *T. Maxey for T. Garthwait*, 1651.

Issued as part of *Herbert's Remains;* see no. 6.

Poemata Varii Argumenti

Wing puts this collection both under Herbert (H.1511) and under Dillingham (D.1484); it is, in fact, by Dillingham but includes a few of Herbert's poems translated into Latin. Not included in the present catalogue.

Priest to the Temple

Prose. On the life and duties of a country parson. Edited by Barnabas Oley (1602–85) who had probably known Herbert at Cambridge. The first edition, 1652, was published as part of 'Herbert's Remains' and not, as far as is known, separately.

A priest to the temple. *T. Maxey for T. Garthwait*, 1652. Issued as part of *Herbert's Remains*; See no. 6.

[4] The second edition; with a new praeface, by B.O. *T. Roycroft, for Benj. Tooke*, 1671. **[Plate 4]**

8⁰. A⁸ a⁸ B–O⁸. (O8 blank.) Paginated (B1) 1–139.

A1 blank. A1ᵛ Imprimatur dated 24 May 1671. A2 title (verso blank). A3 'The Author to the Reader', signed '1632.Geo.Herbert'. A4ᵛ blank. A5 'The Publisher, to the Christian Reader', signed: 'Barnabas Oley'. a7ᵛ blank. a8 contents. B1 text, with HT and initial. K6ᵛ blank. K7 'An Advertisement to the Reader'. K8 'A Prefatory view of the Life and Virtues of the Authour'. O7 list of books sold by Benjamin Tooke (verso blank).

Catchwords: A–a, *wisdome.* a–B, The [A] G–H, hath L–M, (Col-)ledge, [*ledge,*] N–O, *the*

RT (A3ᵛ-A4) *To the Reader.* (A5ᵛ–a7) To the Reader. (a8ᵛ) The Contents. (B1ᵛ–K6) [RT changes with the section headings.] (K7ᵛ) 𝔄𝔫 𝔄𝔡𝔳𝔢𝔯𝔱𝔦𝔰𝔢𝔪𝔢𝔫𝔱 𝔱𝔬 𝔱𝔥𝔢 ℜ𝔢𝔞𝔡𝔢𝔯. (K8/9–O5/6) 𝔒𝔣 𝔱𝔥𝔢 𝔏𝔦𝔣𝔢 𝔬𝔣/𝔐𝔯. G. HERBERT, &c. (O6ᵛ) 𝔒𝔣 𝔱𝔥𝔢 𝔏𝔦𝔣𝔢 𝔬𝔣

BM (1355.b.9.)–O8, wanting O7. Bodl. (110 k 299)–O8. ULC (1)? + O8; (2)–O8. TCD, + O8.
Wing H.1513 (+)

[5] The third impression. *T.R. for Benj Tooke*, 1675.　　**[Plate 5]**

Printer: Thomas Roycroft.

12⁰. A¹² a⁸ B–L¹² M⁴ (L12 blank). Paginated (B1) 1–166.
A1 blank. A1ᵛ Imprimatur as before. A2 title (verso blank). A3 'The Author to
the Reader', signed as before. A4ᵛ blank. A5 'A Preface to the Christian
Reader' signed: 'Barnabas Oley'. a7 contents. a8ᵛ blank. B1 text, with HT.
H12 'An Advertisement to the Reader'. I1 'A Prefatory View of the Life and
Virtues of the Authour'. L12 blank. M1 List of books sold by Benjamin Tooke.

Catchwords: A–a, *by* B–C, over G–H, when K–L, *There*

RT (A3/4) *The Author/to the Reader.* (A5/6) A Preface/to the Reader. (a6ᵛ)
A Preface, &c. (a7/8) The Contents. (B1ᵛ–H11ᵛ) [RT changes with the section
headings.] (H12ᵛ) 𝕬𝖓 𝕬𝖇𝖇𝖊𝖗𝖙𝖎𝖘𝖊𝖒𝖊𝖓𝖙 𝖙𝖔 𝖙𝖍𝖊 𝕽𝖊𝖆𝖉𝖊𝖗. (I1/2–L10/11) 𝕺𝖋 𝖙𝖍𝖊 𝕷𝖎𝖋𝖊
𝖔𝖋/𝕸𝖗. G. HERBERT, &c. (L11ᵛ) 𝕺𝖋 𝖙𝖍𝖊 𝕷𝖎𝖋𝖊 𝖔𝖋, &c.

BM (852.e.10.) + L12. Bodl. (Bliss B 355) + L12, wanting M. Dr. Williams's
Library + L12, wanting a1–8. London University, + L12. Dyce.
Wing H.1514 (+)

Remains

*Comprising the first edition of 'A Priest to the Temple' and a second,
enlarged, edition of 'Outlandish Proverbs' under the title 'Jacula Prudentum.'
Facsimile reprint by Scolar Press, 1970.*

[6] Herbert's remains. Or, sundry pieces. *For Timothy Garthwait*, 1652
　　　　　　　　　　　　　　　　　　　　　　　　　[Plates 6–8]

Printer T. Maxey (See titlepage of *A Priest to the Temple* and *Jacula Prudentum*).
12⁰. A⁶ a–b¹² c⁶ B–H¹². ²A–D¹². Paginated (B1)1–168. (²A2)1–94 (misprinting
71–94 as 171–194).

A1 general title (Plate 6, verso blank). A2 title of 'A Priest to the Temple'
(Plate 7, verso blank). A3 'The Authour to the Reader', signed: 'Geo.Herbert'.
A5 table of contents. On A6 errata. A6ᵛ 'A prefatory view of the life of Mr
Geo.Herbert'. a1 'A prefatory view of the life and vertues of the authour'. B1
text, with HT, lace ornament and initial. ²A1 title of 'Jacula Prudentum'
(Plate 8, verso blank). A2 text, with HT, lace ornament and initial. D1 'The
Authour's Prayer before Sermon'. D3ᵛ 'Mr.G.Herbert, to Master N.F. upon
the Translation of Valdesso'. D5ᵛ 'In Honorem . . . Francisci de Verulamio
Vicecomitis Sti Albani' (in verse). D6ᵛ 'To Doctour Donne upon one of his
Seales' (Latin verse). D7 'An Addition of Apothegmes by Severall Authours'.

Catchwords: a–b, *any* b–c, *that* B–C, &c. E–F, (be–)ne–[nefit] G–H, (offen–)
ding ²A–B,He ²B–C, The

RT (A3ᵛ–A4ᵛ) *To the Reader.* (A5ᵛ–A6) The Contents. (a1/2–c5/6) Of the Life
of/Mr.G.Herbert,&c. (c6ᵛ) Of the Life of (B1–H12) [RT changes with the

17

section headings.] (²A2ᵛ–C12ᵛ) *Jacula Prudentum.* (D1/2) *A Prayer./Before Sermon.* (D2/3) A Prayer/After SERMON. (D7–D12ᵛ) *Apothegmes.*

BM (E.1279); 1070. h.4 (imp. 'Jacula Prudentum' only. Rebound). Bodl. (Mal.376). ULC. Dr. Williams's Library. London University.

Wing H.1515 (+ also 1509 and 1512).

Temple

Poems. Edited posthumously by Herbert's friend Nicholas Ferrar. Textual corrections made in the second to the fifth editions are noted by Hutchinson (cf. pp. lxxvi–vii). Editions after the fifth are not of textual importance. The later editions are often found bound with (and were probably issued with) editions of the anonymous work by Christopher Harvey: 'The Synagogue . . . in Imitation of Mr. George Herbert' (first edition 1640). Facsimile reprint of first edition (1633) by the Scolar Press, Menston, 1968. No entry in SR.

[**7**] The temple. Sacred poems and private ejaculations. *Cambridge: Thom. Buck, and Roger Daniel,* 1633.   [**Plate 9**]

12.⁰ ¶⁴ A–H¹² I.² Paginated (A1) 1–192.
¶1 title (verso blank). ¶2 'The Printers to the Reader'. ¶3ᵛ blank. ¶4 'The dedication' (6 ll. verse. Verso blank). A1 text headed 'The Church-porch', with lace ornament and initial. I1 'The titles of the severall poems contained in this book' (verso blank).

Catchwords: A–B,They B–C, ¶Employ-[¶Employment.] E–F, For G12–G12ᵛ, ¶Mary [¶Marie] G–H,Onely

A9 (p. 17) [Lace ornament at head and foot of page, title and text not enclosed in frame.] A9ᵛ (p. 18) [Lace ornament at head and foot of page, text not enclosed in rules.] I1 The titles of the severall poems/contained in this book.

RT (A1ᵛ–A8ᵛ) *The Church-Porch.* (A9ᵛ–H8) *The Church.* (H9–H12) *The Church Militant.*

BM (C.58.a.26). London University. ULC.

STC 13183 (+) Hutchinson 1a.

[**7a**] [The same sheets with a cancel title.] *Cambridge, Thomas Buck and Roger Daniel; sold by Francis Green.* [1633.]   [**Plate 10**]

Bodl. (Mason CC 87).
STC 13184 (+) Hutchinson 1b.

[8] The second edition. [*Cambridge:*] *T. Buck, and R. Daniel,* 1633.
[**Plate 11**]

Collation and contents as in no. 7. Catchwords as in no. 7, except: G12–G12ᵛ, ¶Marie RT as in no. 7

A9 (p. 17) [Lace ornament at head and foot of page, title and text not enclosed in frame.] A9ᵛ (p. 18) [Lace ornament at head and foot of page, text not enclosed in rules.] I1 THE/TITLES OF THE SEVE-/RALL POEMS CONTAIN-/ED IN THIS BOOK.

Bodl. (Mason FF477)

STC 13185 (+ not differentiated from no. 8a). Hutchinson 2a.

[8a] [A variant, with imprint:] [*Cambridge:*] *T. Buck, and R. Daniel;* sold by Fr. Green, 1633.
[**Plate 12**]

BM (1076.i.25). Corpus Christi College, Oxford. ULC.

STC 13185 (not differentiated from no. 8). Hutchinson 2b.

[9] The third edition. [*Cambridge:*] *T. Buck, and R. Daniel;* sold by *Fr. Green,* 1634.
[**Plate 13**]

Collation as in no. 8. Contents as in no. 8, except: A1 has HP instead of lace ornament. Catchwords as in no. 8. RT as in no. 8.

A9 (p. 17). [Lace ornament at head and foot of page, title and text not enclosed in frame.] A9ᵛ (p. 18) [Text enclosed by rules.] I1 [As in no. 8]

BM (1077.b.23). Bodl. (147. g.614). ULC.

STC 13186 (+) Hutchinson 3.

[10] The fourth edition. [*Cambridge:*] *T. Buck, and R. Daniel,* 1635.
[**Plate 14**]

Collation as in no. 9. Contents as in no. 9, except: A1 has lace ornament instead of HP. Catchwords as in no. 9, except: B–C, ¶Employ-[§Employment.] RT as in 9.

A9 (p. 17). [Heading and text completely enclosed in a frame of lace ornament and rules to resemble an arched doorway.] A9ᵛ (p. 18) [Text enclosed by rules.] I1 [As in no. 9]

BM 1077.b.24. Bodl. (Wood 93). London University. ULC.

STC 13187 (+) Hutchinson 4.

[11] The fifth edition. [*Cambridge:*] *T. Buck, and R. Daniel,* 1638.
[**Plate 15**]

Collation, contents and catchwords as in no. 10, except: B–C, ¶Employ-[¶Employment.] RT as in no. 10 except (A1ᵛ–A8ᵛ) *The Church-porch.*

19

A9 (p. 17) [Heading and text completely enclosed in a frame of lace ornament and rules to resemble an arched doorway.] A9ᵛ (p. 18) [Text enclosed by rules.] I1 THE/TITLES OF THE SEVE-/RALL POEMS CONTAINED/IN THIS BOOK.

BM. (11626.a.25.) Bodl. (147.g.342). ULC.

STC 13188 (+) Hutchinson 5.

[**12**] The sixth edition. [*Cambridge:*] *Roger Daniel*, 1641.   [**Plate 16**]

Collation as in no. 11, except: (misprinting E3 as B3). Contents as in no. 11, except: ¶2 'The Printer [singular] . . .' Catchwords as in no. 11, except: G12–G12ᵛ, ¶Marie [¶Mary]. RT as in no. 11, except: (H9–12) *The Church Militant* (*militant*).

A9 (p. 17) [Heading and text completely enclosed in a frame of lace ornament and rules to resemble an arched doorway.] A9ᵛ p. 18) [Text enclosed by rules.] I1 The titles of the severall/poems contained in this/book.

BM (C.128.a.12); (C.128.a.9). Bodl. (147.g.615/1). ULC.

Wing H.1516 (+) Hutchinson 6.

[**13**] The seventh edition. [*n.p.*, 1647?]   [**Plate 17**]

Printed at London by John Leggatt for Philemon Stephens.

Collation as in no. 12, except: (misprinting p. 129 as 139). Contents as in no. 12 except: A1 no initial. Catchwords as in no. 12, except: B–C, ¶Em-[Employment.] G12–G12ᵛ, Marie [¶Mary]. RT as in no. 11.

A9 (p. 17). [Heading and text enclosed in a rectangular frame of lace ornament and rules not in the form of an arch.] A9 (p. 18) [Text enclosed by rules.] I1 The titles of the severall/Poems contained in this/Book.

BM (11626.aa.12). Bodl. (147.g.616)

Wing H.1517 (+) Hutchinson 7. Wing follows the old BM catalogue entry which gives: [Cambridge? 1656.], but typographical evidence shows the printer to be John Legatt of London, and, as Hutchinson suggests (pp. lix–lx), this edition was probably intended to be issued with the second edition of Harvey's *The Synagogue* printed by Legatt for Philemon Stephens in 1647.

[**14**] The seventh edition, with an alphabeticall table. *T.R. for Philemon Stephens*, 1656.   [**Plate 18**]

Printer: Thomas Roycroft. Set up from the 6th ed.

12⁰. *⁶ A–I¹² K⁶ (misprinting E3 as B3, H4 as D4). Paginated (A1) 1–192 (misprinting 187 as 178).

*1 title (verso blank). *2 'The Printer to the Reader'. *4 'The Dedication' (6 ll. verse, verso blank). *5 'The Titles of the several poems'. *6ᵛ blank. A1 text, headed 'The Church-Porch', with lace ornament and initial. I1 table. K6ᵛ blank.

Catchwords as in no. 13, except: B–C, Employ- [¶Employment.] G12–12ᵛ
¶Mary [Mary] RT as in no. 13, except: (A1ᵛ–A8ᵛ) *The Church-Porch.* (I1ᵛ–K6)
A Table.

A9 (p. 17) ¶Superliminare. [Heading and text enclosed in a frame of lace
ornament and rules to resemble an arched doorway.] A9ᵛ (p. 18) ¶The alter.
[Text enclosed by rules.] *5 The Titles of the several/Poems contained in this/
Book.

BM (11626.a.26/1). Bodl. (8⁰A 151 Art.). ULC. TCD.

Wing H 1518 (+) Hutchinson 8.

[**15**] The eighth edition, with an alphabeticall table. *R.N. for Philemon
Stephens*, 1660.   **[Plate 19]**

Printer: Roger Norton?

Collation as in no. 14, correcting the misprints but misprinting p. 87 as 78.
Contents as in no. 14. Catchwords as in no. 14, except: B–C, Employ- [¶Employ-
ment.] G12–12ᵛ, Mary G–H, Only [Onely] RT as in no. 14.

A9 (p. 17) ¶Superliminare. [Heading and text enclosed in a frame of lace
ornament and rules to resemble an arched doorway.] A9ᵛ (p. 18) ¶The Altar.
[Text enclosed by rules.] *5 The Titles of the several/Poems contained in this/
Book.

BM (11626.a.27/1). Bodl. (147.g.177). ULC.

Wing H.1519 (+) Hutchinson 9.

[**16**] The ninth edition, with an alphabetical table. *J.M. for Philemon
Stephens*, 1667.   **[Plate 20]**

Collation as in no. 15, correcting the misprint but misprinting p. 109 as 106.
Contents as in no. 15, except: A1 initial replaced by factotum. Catchwords as
in no. 15, except: B–C, ¶Employ- [¶Employment.] RT as in no. 15
A9 (p. 17) [Heading and text enclosed in an arch formed of rules only, without
lace ornament.] A9ᵛ (p. 18) [Text enclosed by rules.] *5 The Titles of the
several/Poems contained in this/Book.

Bodl. (147.g.637); (Vet.A3 f 773). Magdalen College, Oxford. Dr. Williams's
Library (*imp.*) ULC. TCD.

Wing H.1520 (+) Hutchinson 10.

[**16a**] [A variant, with imprint:] *J.M. for Philemon Stephens, and J.
Stephens*, 1667.   **[Plate 21]**

BM (11626.aa.13/1).
Not in Wing. Mentioned by Hutchinson in his no. 10.

[17] [Another edition.] The Temple . . . By Mr.George Herbert . . .
Together with his Life . . . The tenth edition, with an alphabetical
table. *W. Godbid, for R.S.; sold by John Williams junior,* 1674.
[Plate 22]

Publisher: Robert Stephens. An important edition for its new preliminary
matter, including Walton's Life reproduced with small changes from his
Lives (1670), and the engraved portrait by R. White.

12°.π⁶ πA–B¹² C⁶*⁶ (–*1). A–I¹² K⁶. (Misprinting *3 as *4, B4 as B2). Paginated
(πA1)1–60. (A1)1–192.

π1 blank. π1ᵛ portrait. π2 title (verso blank). π3 'These Lines should have
been under his Picture' (8 ll. verse, verso blank). π4 'A Memorial to . . .
George Herbert' (in verse followed by 'An Epitaph upon . . . George Herbert'
in verse, signed: 'P.D.', and 'The Church Militant' in verse). *1 cancelled. *2
'The Printer to the Reader'. *4 'The Dedication' (6 ll. verse, verso blank). *5
'The Titles of the several Poems'. *6ᵛ blank. A1 Walton's Life of Herbert. A1
text, headed 'The Church-Porch', with lace ornament. I1 table. K6ᵛ blank.
It is probable that all the new preliminary matter (π1–πC6), including Walton's
Life, has been added as an afterthought and substituted for the original title
(*1). In some copies the order is transposed, * following π and the Life (πA1–
C6) either preceding the poems and table (A1–K6) or following them. Many
copies are found bound with the 6th edition (1673) of Harvey's *The Synagogue*
which is sometimes inserted between the poems and table and the Life.

Catchwords: as in no. 16 except: B–C, ¶Em- [¶Employment.] G12–G12ᵛ,
¶Mary [¶Mary-Magdalen.]   G–H, Only

RT (πA1/2–πC5/6) 𝕿𝖍𝖊 𝕷𝕴𝕵𝕰 of / 𝕸𝖗. 𝕲𝖊𝖔𝖗𝖌𝖊 𝕳𝖊𝖗𝖇𝖊𝖗𝖙. (A1ᵛ–A8) *The
CHURCH-PORCH.* (A9ᵛ–H8) *The CHURCH.* (H9–12) *The CHURCH
MILITANT.* (I1ᵛ–K6) A TABLE.

A8ᵛ (p. 16) Engraving of a church porch, with the text, engraved, beneath.
A9 (p. 17) Engraving of an altar, forming a frame in which the text, engraved,
is enclosed. *5 The TITLES of the several/POEMS contained in this/Book.

BM (11623.aa.15/1) wanting the Life; (G.18857) wanting the Life. Bodl.
(Mason FF 475) wanting π1; (Vet.A3f 1230) wanting π1. London University.
Dyce. ULC.

Wing H.1521 (+) Hutchinson 11.

[18] The eleventh edition, with an alphabetical table. *S. Roycroft, for
R.S.; sold by John Williams junior,* 1678.   **[Plate 23]**

12⁰. πA¹² 2πA–B¹² C⁶ A–I¹² K.⁶ (Misprinting 2πA4 as A3. πA1, 2 blank.
2πC⁶ blank. In some copies the portrait is pasted onto the verso of πA2, in others
πA2 is cancelled and the portrait inserted in its place.) Paginated (2πA1)
1–158. (A1) 1–192.

πA3 title (verso blank). πA4 'These Lines should have been under his picture'
(as before, verso blank). πA5 'A Memorial . . .' (as before). πA8 'The Printer to
the Reader'. πA10 'The Dedication' (as before, verso blank). πA11 'The Titles

of the several Poems'. πA12ᵛ blank. ²πA1 'The Life of Mr.George Herbert' by Isaak Walton. A1 text headed 'The Church-Porch', with lace ornament. I1 table. K6ᵛ blank.

Catchwords as in no. 17 except: B–C, Em- [¶Employment.]

RT (²πA2/3–C3/4) 𝕿𝖍𝖊 𝕷𝕴𝕱𝕰 of/𝕸r. 𝕲eorge 𝕳erbert. (²πC4ᵛ) 𝕿𝖍𝖊 𝕷𝕴𝕱𝕰 of (A1ᵛ–A8ᵛ) *The CHURCH-PORCH.* (A9–H8) *The CHURCH.* (H8ᵛ–H12) *The CHURCH MILITANT.* (I1ᵛ–K6) A TABLE.

A8ᵛ (p. 16) Engraving of a church porch, with the text, engraved, beneath. A9 (p. 17) Engraving of an altar, forming a frame in which the text, engraved, is enclosed. A11 The TITLES of the several/POEMS contained in this/Book.

Many copies of this edition are found bound with editions of *The Synagogue.*

Bodl. (14470.f.587)–πA2 including the portrait, + ²πC6.

Wing H.1522 (+) Hutchinson 12a.

[18a] [A variant with date:] 167.9 [*sic*.]   **[Plate 24]**

BM (852.e.9)–πA1, ²πC6, with the portrait pasted onto πA2ᵛ; (238.e.43) + A1, ²πC6, with πA2 cancelled and the portrait inserted in its place. Bodl. (147.g.617)+πA1, ²πC6, with the portrait pasted onto πA2ᵛ. ULC.

Wing H.1523 (+) Hutchinson 12b.

[19] The eleventh edition, with an alphabetical table. *For R.S.; sold by Richard Willington,* 1695.   **[Plate 25]**

A reissue of the sheets of the tenth edition (no. 17) from sig. *2 onwards. The preliminaries before sig. *2 are the same as those of the tenth edition but reprinted.

[Preliminaries:] 8⁰. π1 ²π4 (π1 blank, with the portrait pasted onto the verso). ²π1 title (verso blank). ²π2 'A Memorial to . . . George Herbert [as before]' On ²π4 'These Lines should have been under his Picture'. *1 cancelled.

Bodl. (Vet.A3 f.1077) London University.

Wing H.1524 (+) Hutchinson 13.

CRASHAW

CRASHAW, Richard. (1612–49)

Son of William Crashaw the Puritan writer. Went to Pembroke College, Cambridge, in 1631, became a fellow of Peterhouse c.1635, ordained in the Anglican church, and was closely associated with Nicholas Ferrar and the Little Gidding community. He left Cambridge during the civil war and was ejected from his fellowship. He became a Catholic c.1645. He was in Paris in 1646 where he was helped by Cowley; in the same year he went to Rome with a recommendation from Henrietta Maria to the Pope, but was reduced to living in great poverty. In 1647 he was in the service of Cardinal Palotta by whose favour he was given a canonry at Loreto where he died two years later.

Chronology of the Publication of Crashaw's Works to 1700

1634. *Epigrammatum sacrorum liber.* [Latin epigrams. Printed at Cambridge while Crashaw was still resident there.]

1646. *Steps to the temple.* [A collection of poems, some in Latin some in English, in two parts, sacred and secular, the first entitled 'Sacred Poems', the second 'Delights of the Muses'. Preface by an unknown editor. Printed at London. Crashaw was already abroad when it appeared.]

1648. *Steps to the temple . . . The second edition.* [With several new poems added and several old ones amplified. Printed at London.]

1652. *Carmen Deo nostro . . . Sacred poems.* [Another edition of 'Sacred Poems' in *Steps to the temple*, based on the 1648 edition but adding some new poems. A posthumous publication probably edited by Crashaw's friend Miles Pinkney, alias Thomas Car, who contributes two prefatory poems. Printed at Paris.]

1653. *A letter to the Countess of Denbigh.* [A single poem. A longer version, with many textual differences, of the poem of this title first printed in *Carmen Deo nostro*, 1652. Printed at London.]

1670. *Richardi Crashawi poemata et epigrammata . . . Editio secunda.* [An enlarged edition of the 1634 *Epigrammatum sacrorum liber*, with the addition of Latin poems (the 'Poemata') taken from the 1646 edition of *Steps to the temple*. Printed at Cambridge.]

1670. *Steps to the temple, . . . The 2d edition.* [A reprint of *Steps to the temple*, 1646, and *Carmen Deo nostro*, 1652. The unknown editor probably unaware of the existence of the real second edition of 1648. Printed at London.]

27

1674. *Richardi Crashawi poemata et epigrammata.* [A reissue, with a cancel title of the edition of 1670.]

1688. *Epigrammata sacra selecta.* [Selections from *Epigrammatum sacrorum liber*, with translations into English verse by Clement Barksdale.]

[c.1690.] *Steps to the temple.* [A reissue of the 1670 edition with a cancel title.]

Carmen Deo Nostro

See no. 8.

Delights of the Muses

See nos. 6, 7, 9, 10.

Epigrammata Sacra

See no. 4.

Epigrammatum Sacrorum Liber

Latin epigrams. The first edition was printed at Cambridge while Crashaw was still resident there and he may have seen it through the press; the second, with additions and emendations, appeared twenty years after his death. No entry in SR.

[**1**] Epigrammatum sacrorum liber. *Cantabrigiae, ex Academiae celeberrimae typographeo,* 1634.   [**Plate 1**]

Anon.

8^0. ¶^{8} A–E.^{8} Paginated (A1) 1–79.

¶1 title (verso blank). ¶2 'Reverendo admodum viro, Benjamino Lany . . . ex suorum minimis minimus R.C.' (prose and verse). ¶4^v 'Venerabili viro Magistro Tournay' (verse). ¶5 'Ornatissimo viro . . . Magistro Brook' (verse). ¶5^v Lectori' (verse and prose). ¶8^v blank. A1 text, with HT, lace ornament and initial. E8^v blank.

Catchwords: A–B, Luc.2. C–D, *Laudem* D–E, ACT.

RT (A1^v–E8) Epigrammata Sacra.

BM (11409.c.20). Bodl. (8^0 E 76 Th.) ULC.

STC 6009 (+) Martin 1.

[2] [Another edition.] Richardi Crashawi poemata et epigrammata . . . Editio secunda, auctior & emendatior. *Cantabrigiae, ex officina Joan. Hayes,* 1670. **[Plate 2]**

The 'Poemata' of this edition have been added from the 1648 edition of *Steps to the Temple.* To the 'Epigrammata' of 1634 some new Latin epigrams and several Greek versions have been added.

8⁰. A–F⁸. Paginated (B7) 1–67.

A1 title (verso blank). A2 'Reverendo admodum viro Benjamino Lany . . . ex suorum minimis minimus R. Crashaw' (prose and verse). A4 'Venerabili viro Magistro Tournay' (verse). A4ᵛ 'Ornatissimo viro . . . Magistro Brook' (verse). A5 text of Poemata, without HT, beginning 'In picturam Reverendissimi Episcopi, D. Andrews'. B3 title of Epigrammata Sacra. B3ᵛ 'Lectori'. B6ᵛ text of Epigrammata Sacra, with HT, lace ornament and initial. F8ᵛ blank.

Catchwords: A–B, *O ţia* B–C, ACT. C–D, *Cur* D–E, JOANN. E–F, MATTH.

RT (B7–F8) Epigrammata Sacra.

BM (237.c.35). Bodl. (Douce CC 29/1) ULC.

Wing C. 6834 (+). Martin 6.

[3] [Another issue, with a cancel title.] *Cantabrigae, ex officina Joan. Hayes; prostant venales apud Joann. Creed,* 1674. **[Plate 3]**

Bodl. (Vet A3 f818). ULC.

Wing C. 6835 (+) Martin 8.

[3a] [A variant cancel title.] **[Plate 4]**

Magdalen College, Oxford.

[4] Epigrammata sacra selecta, cum Anglica versione. Sacred epigrams Englished. *London, for John Barksdale, book-seller in Cirencester,* 1682. **[Plate 5]**

Anon. Selections from Crashaw's *Epigrammatum sacrorum liber,* with translations into English verse, probably by Clement Barksdale, the West country poet, (?) brother of the bookseller.

8⁰. A⁸. (A1 blank?) Paginated (A3) 3–13.

A2 title (verso blank) A3 text, with HT. A8ᵛ blank.

Catchwords: A3–4, *Stay* A5–6, 23. In A7–8, *This*

No RT

Bodl. (Vet. A3. f. 270/2)–A1. (This was Bliss's copy, with his note about Clement Barksdale.)

Wing C. 6832 (listing the Huntington copy only).

Letter to the Countess of Denbigh

A single poem. A longer version, with many textual differences, of the poem of this title first published in 'Carmen Deo Nostro', 1652.

[5] A letter . . . to the Countess of Denbigh. *London* [1653].

[Plate 6]

> 4⁰. A². Paginated (A1ᵛ) 1–3.
>
> A1 title. A1ᵛ text, with HT 'Against Irresolution and Delay in matters of Religion' and initial (factotum).
>
> Catchwords: A1–2, Seed- [Seed-time's]   A2–A2ᵛ, Spurns
>
> No RT.
>
> BM (E.220/2). (The date 1653 is added in ink in a contemporary hand (not Thomason's); Thomason has added 'Sept: 23' above the year.)
>
> Wing C. 6833 (listing this copy only). Martin 5.

Poemata et Epigrammata

See nos. 2–3a.

Sacred Poems

See nos. 6–10.

Steps to the Temple

A collection of poems in two parts, sacred and secular, the first entitled 'Sacred Poems', the second 'Delights of the Muses'. Entered in SR 1 June 1646. Assigned by the widow of Humphrey Moseley to Henry Herringman, 19 Aug. 1667. Re-entered to Herringman, 2 Dec. 1669.

[6] Steps to the temple. Sacred poems, with other delights of the muses. *T.W. for Humphrey Moseley*, 1646.   **[Plate 7]**

> Crashaw had been in Paris for some time when the edition appeared and he did not see it through the press. The preface by an unknown editor speaks of him as 'now dead to us'.
>
> 12⁰. A⁶ B–G¹². (A1, G12 blank).   Paginated (B1) 1–138.
>
> A2 title (verso blank). A3 'The Preface to the Reader'. A6 'The Authors Motto' (2 ll. verse). A6ᵛ 'Reader, there was a sudden mistake . . .' B1 text, with lace ornament and initial. F2ᵛ blank. F3 title of The Delights of the Muses (verso blank). F4 text of The Delights of the Muses. G10 table.

Catchwords: B–C, *Psalme*. [*Psalme*] C–D, *Loves* D–E, Make F–G, out [Ad]
RT (A3/4–A4/5) The Preface /To the Reader. (A5ᵛ) To the Reader. (B1ᵛ–F2)
Steps to the Temple. (F4ᵛ–G9ᵛ) The Delights of the Muses. (G10–G11ᵛ) The
Table.

BM (E.1154/1.) Bodl. (Douce C96)–A1, +G12. Trinity College Cambridge,
+A1, G12.

Wing C. 6836 (+) Martin 2.

[7] Steps to the temple, sacred poems. With the delights of the
muses . . . The second edition. *For Humphrey Moseley*, 1648.
[Plate 8]

Crawshaw had been absent from England for three years when the edition
appeared. Several new poems are added and several old ones amplified. The
unamplified old poems are set up from the 1646 edition.

12⁰. π1 A⁶ B–F¹² ²A–C¹². Paginated (B1) 1–113. (²A1) 1–71.

π1 engraved title (verso blank). A1 printed title (verso blank). A2 'The Preface
to the Reader'. A4ᵛ 'The Authors Motto' (2 ll verse). A5 table to The
Delights of the Muses. A6ᵛ blank. B1 text, with lace ornament and initial.
F9ᵛ blank. F10 table to Steps to the Temple. F11ᵛ blank. F12 title of The
Delights of the Muses (verso blank). ²A1 text of The Delights of the Muses.
²C12 blank.

Catchwords: B–C, Mat. C–D, *Chorus*. D–E, 62. So ²A–B, The ²B–C, *To*
RT (A2/3–A3/4) The Preface (Preface.)/To the Reader. (A5ᵛ–A6) The Table.
(B1ᵛ–F9) Steps to the Temple. (F10ᵛ–F11ᵛ) The Table. (²A1ᵛ–C12) The
Delights of the Muses.

BM (1482.aa.11); (E.1152/2), with A5, 6 the table to Delights of the Muses
bound at the end, after C12, wanting π1. Bodl. (8⁰ H16 Th. BS/2) A5, 6 in
right place; (Douce C442) A5, 6 at end. ULC.

Wing C. 6837/6831 (+). Martin 3.

[8] [Another edition of 'Sacred Poems' only.] Carmen Deo nostro . . .
Sacred poems. *Paris, Peter Targa*, 1652. **[Plate 9]**

Crashaw was dead when this edition appeared. It was probably seen through
the press by his friend Miles Pinkney alias Thomas Car, chaplain to the English
Augustinian nuns at Paris. It contains some new poems but consists mainly
of poems first printed in 1648, or first printed then in altered or expanded form.

8⁰ (in 4s). a⁴ A–Q⁴ R² (misprinting C3 as C2). Paginated (A1) 1–130.

a1 title (verso blank). a2 'Crashawe, the Anagramme . . .' (verse). a3 'An
Epigramme' (verse), signed: 'Thomas Car'. a3ᵛ poem 'To the . . . Countesse
of Denbigh'. A1 text, with engraved emblem and initial. R2ᵛ blank.

Catchwords: a–A, TO C–D, Waery [Weary] G–H, Each F–G, THE
[VEXILLA] N–O, Giue Q–R, If it
RT (A1/2–R1/2) SACRED (SACRET)/POEMS.

BM (E.1598/1); (G.11497); (238.g.8) in this copy spaces are left for the engravings. Bodl. (Douce CC 233) the engraving on K4. is different from that in the BM copies.

Wing C. 6830 (+). Martin 4.

[9] [Another edition of the whole.] Steps to the temple, the delights of the muses, and carmen Deo nostro . . . The 2d edition. *In the Savoy, T.N. for Henry Herringman*, 1670.   **[Plate 10]**

A reprint of the texts of 1646 and 1652. The publishers were perhaps unaware of the genuine second edition of 1648.

8⁰. π1 A–O⁸ (o8 blank). Paginated (B1) 1–208 (omitting 113–14, misprinting 180–1 as 182–3, 184–5 as 186–7, 188–9 as 190–1, 192–3 as 194–5).

π1 engraved title (verso blank). A1 printed title (verso blank). A2 'The Preface to the Reader'. A5ᵛ 'The Authors Motto' (2 ll. verse). A6 table. B1 text, with lace ornament and initial. F7ᵛ blank. F8 title of The Delights of the Muses (verso blank). G1 text of The Delights of the Muses, with HT and lace ornament. K4ᵛ blank. K5 title of Carmen Deo Nostro (verso blank). K6 text of Carmen Deo Nostro, with lace ornament.

Catchwords: B–C, *Luk*. [Luk.] D–E, 47. Scarce G–H, *Vpon* [*Upon*] N–O, Why

RT (A2/3–A4/5) The Preface/to the Reader. (A6ᵛ–A8ᵛ) The TABLE. (B1ᵛ–F7) *Steps to the Temple*. (G1ᵛ–K4) *The Delights of the Muses*. (K6ᵛ) *The Delights of the Muses*. (K7ᵛ–O7ᵛ) *Sacred Poems*.

BM (G.18869) + O8; (238.h.23)–O8. Bodl. (Douce CC29/2)–O8. Magdalen College, Oxford, O8 partly torn away.

Wing C. 6839 (+). 6838 appears to be a 'ghost'. Martin 7.

[10] [A reissue, with a cancel title.] The third edition. *For Richard Bently, Jacob Tonson, Francis Saunders, and Tho. Bennet* [c.1690].
          [Plate 11]

The date must be between about 1687, when Bennet, the last of the four to set up in business, began issuing books with his imprint, and about 1697 when Bently died.

Hunt.

Wing C. 6840 (listing this copy only). Martin 9.

VAUGHAN

VAUGHAN, Henry (1621–95)

Born in Breconshire, of Welsh descent, the twin brother of Thomas whose interest in alchemy he shared. Went to Jesus College, Oxford, but left the university without taking a degree. In London in 1640, left in 1642 on the outbreak of civil war, married and settled at Newton in Breconshire c.1646. Spent most of the rest of his life in Breconshire where he devoted himself to his literary work and country pursuits.

Chronology of the Publication of Vaughan's Works to 1700

1646.   *Poems, with the tenth satyre of Juvenal Englished.* [Secular poems.]
1650.   *Silex scintillans: or sacred poems and private ejaculations.* [Religious poems.]
1651.   *Olor Iscanus. A collection of some select poems and translations.* Secular poems, followed by three translations in prose.]
1652.   *The Mount of Olives: or, solitary devotions.* [Meditations in prose. With a translation of a work attributed to St. Anselm of Canterbury: *De Felicitate Sanctorum*, to which Vaughan gives the title: *Man in Glory.*]
1654.   *Flores solitudinis. Certaine rare and elegant pieces.* [Prose translations from Nieremberg and Eucherius and from an anonymous life of Paulinus of Nola.]
1655.   *Silex scintillans . . . The second edition.* [A reissue of the 1650 edition, with the addition of a second part not previously published.]
1655.   *Hermetical physick.* [Prose. A translation of a work by the alchemical writer Henricus Nollius: *Systema Medicinae Hermeticae Generalis.*]
1657.   *The chymists key to shut, and to open.* [Prose. A translation of Nollius: *De Generatione Rerum Naturalium.*]
1678.   *Thalia rediviva. The pass-time and diversions of a countrey-muse.* [Secular poems, including verse translations from Boethius and Claudian.]
1679.   *Olor Iscanus* [A reissue, with a cancel title, of the 1651 edition.]

Anselm, of Canterbury, Saint. (Translation of a work attributed to him.)

See no. 4.

Chymists Key

A translation of Henricus Nollius, 'De Generatione Rerum Naturalium'. The translation, which is anonymous, has sometimes been attributed to Henry Vaughan's brother Thomas, but Henry claims it as his own in a letter to Aubrey of 15 June 1673 (cf. Martin, p. 754). No entry in SR.

[1] The chymists key to shut, and to open. *E.B. for L. Lloyd*, 1657.
[Plate 1]

12⁰. A⁶ B–C¹² D⁶ E². Paginated (B1) 1–63.

A1 title (verso blank). A2 'To the Reader' signed: 'Eugenius Philalethes'. B1 text, with HP and initial. E2ᵛ blank.

Catchwords: A3–4, incor- [*incorporating*] B–C, in C–D, moysten

RT (A2ᵛ–A6ᵛ) To the READER. (B1ᵛ–E2ʳ) *The Chymists Key.*
Christ Church, Oxford.

Wing N. 1221 (+). Martin 8.

Eucherius, Saint (Translation from)

See no. 2.

Flores Solitudinis

Prose pieces, comprising translations from Nieremberg 'De Arte Voluntatis', Eucherius 'De Contemptu Mundi' and an anonymous Latin life of Paulinus of Nola. Entered in SR 15 September 1653.

[2] Flores solitudinis. Certaine rare and elegant pieces. *Humphrey Moseley*, 1654. [Plate 2]

12⁰. π² A⁴ χ⁴ B–I¹² ²A–G¹² (misprinting C4 as B4; ²G12 blank). Paginated (B1ᵛ) 2–191, (²A2) 3–165.

π1 title (verso blank). π2 title of 'Two Excellent Discourses . . . by Johan: Euseb: Nierembergius' (verso blank). A1 'To . . . Sir Charles Egerton Knight', signed: 'Henry Vaughan' and dated: 'Newton by Uske near Sketh-Rock 1653'. A4ᵛ blank. χ1 'To the onely true and glorious God . . .' in verse. χ2 'To the Reader', in prose, signed: 'Hen: Vaughan', and dated: 'Newton by Usk . . . April. 17. 1652'. B1 text, with HT 'Of Temperance and Patience', lace ornament and initial. G1ᵛ text of 'Of Life and Death'. I12ᵛ blank. ²A1 title of 'The World Contemned . . . by Eucherius' (verso blank). ²A2 'Advertisement', signed: 'H.V.S.' ²A3 text, with HT, lace ornament and initial. ²C4ᵛ blank. ²C5 title of 'Primitive Holiness' (verso blank). ²C6 'To the Reader', signed: 'H.V.' ²C7 text, with HT, lace ornament and initial. ²G8ᵛ blank. ²G9 'St. Paulinus to his Wife Therasia', in verse. ²G11ᵛ blank.

Catchwords: B–C, the E–F, There- [Therefore] G–H, Mur- [murther] ²C–D, *Cri-* [*Crimen*] ²F–G, The

No RT.

BM (856.a.12)–²G12, wanting χ2, 3, prelims rebound in different order. Bodl. (8⁰ F2 Th.BS/2) + ²G12. Christ Church, Oxford, +²G12, prelims rebound in different order. ULC, –²G12.

Wing V. 121 (+). Martin 5.

Guevara, Antonio de (Translation from)

See nos. 5, 6.

Hermetical Physick

A translation of Henricus Nollius, 'Systema Medicinae Hermeticae Generalis'. Entered in SR 16 January 1654/5.

[3] Hermetical physick . . . Englished by Henry Uaughan. *For Humphrey Moseley,* 1655. **[Plate 3]**

12⁰. A⁴ B–F¹² G⁶ (G6 blank. Misprinting A3 as A5, B4 as B7). Paginated (B1) 1–130.

A1 title (verso blank). A2 'The Translator to the ingenious Reader'. A4ᵛ 'Plautus. Qui mali sunt, habeant mala . . .' B1 text, with HT, lace ornament and initial.

Catchwords: A–B, Her- [HERMETICALL] C–D, most E–F, (an-)other, F–G, apply

RT (A2ᵛ–A4ᵛ) *To the Reader.* (B1ᵛ–G5ᵛ) *Hermetical Physick.*

BM (E.1714/1) + G6. Bodl. (8⁰ A30 Med. Bs.) + G6.

Wing N. 1222 (+) Martin 7. (+)

Juvenal, Decimus Junius (Translation from)

See no. 7.

Man in Glory

See no. 4.

Mount of Olives

Meditations in prose. With a translation of a work attributed to St. Anselm of Canterbury: 'De Felicitate Sanctorum', to which Vaughan gives the title: 'Man in Glory'. Entered in SR 16 December 1651.

[4] The mount of olives: or, solitary devotions. *For William Leake,* 1652. **[Plate 4]**

12⁰. A–I¹² (A1 blank except for woodcut crown on verso. I12 blank. Misprinting B5 as R5). Paginated (B1) 1–189 (misprinting 72 as 48, 83 as 59, and omitting 169–70).

A1 blank. A1ᵛ blank except for woodcut crown. A2 title (verso blank). A3 'To . . . Sr Charles Egerton knight', signed: 'Vaughan' and dated Newton by Usk, 1 October 1651. A6ᵛ blank. A7 'To the Peaceful . . . Reader', signed: 'Henry Vaughan'. A10ᵛ blank. A11 table. A12ᵛ blank except for woodcut crown. B1 text, headed 'Admonitions for Morning-Prayer', with lace ornament and initial. G6ᵛ blank. G7 title of 'Man in Glory' (verso blank). G8 address to the reader, signed: 'Hen. Vaughan'. G9ᵛ 12 ll. verse. G10 'Revel. Chap. 7. G11 text of 'Man in Glory'. I10ᵛ 'Books Printed or sold by William Leake'. I11ᵛ blank.

Catchwords: B–C, the   D–E, It   F–G, and H–I, *Jesus*

RT (A3/4–A5/6) *The Epistle/Dedicatory*. (A7–A10) To the Reader. (A11ᵛ–A12) The TABLE. (B1/2–G5/6) *The Mount of Olives,/or Solitary Devotions*. (G8–9) *To the Reader*. (G10–I10) *Man in Glory*.

BM (E.1305/2) + A1, I12. Bodl. (I g. 124)–A1, I12, wants I11, with variant RT (G8ᵛ) *Man in Glory*. (G10ᵛ) *To the Reader*.

Wing V. 122 (+). Martin 4.

Nieremberg, Juan Eusebio (Translations from)

See no. 2.

Nollius, Henricus (Translations from)

See nos. 1, 3.

Of the Diseases of the Mind and the Body

See nos. 5, 6.

Olor Iscanus

Secular poems, followed by four translations in prose. The first two, 'Of the Benefit, wee may get by our Enemies' and 'Of the Diseases of the Mind and the Body' are from Latin versions by John Reynolds of the original Greek of Plutarch (cf. Martin, p. 95). The third, also entitled 'Of the

Diseases of the Mind and the Body', is from a Latin version by Reynolds of the Greek of Maximus Tirius. The fourth, entitled 'The Praise and Happinesse of the Countrie-Life' is from Guevara's 'Menosprecio de Corte'. Entered in SR 28 April 1651.

[5] Olor Iscanus. A collection of some select poems, and translations. T.W. for Humphrey Moseley, 1651.   [Plate 5]

8⁰. A–L⁸ χ1. (L8 blank?) Paginated (B1) 1–158 (repeating 91, omitting 93). A1 blank. A1ᵛ 'Ad Posteros' verse. A2 blank. A2ᵛ engraved title. A3 printed title. A3ᵛ two lines from Vergil beginning 'O quis me gelidis in vallibus Iscae...' A4 'To ... Lord Kildare Digby', signed: 'Vaughan' and dated from Newton by Usk, 17 December 1647. A6 'The Publisher to the Reader'. A7 'Vpon the most Ingenious pair of Twins', in verse, signed: 'T. Powell Oxoniensis'. A7ᵛ 'To my friend the Authour', signed: 'I. Rowlandson Oxoniensis'. A8 'Vpon the following Poems', signed: 'Eugenius Philalethes Oxoniensis'. B1 text, with HT and lace ornament. F1 title of 'Of the Benefit wee may get by our Enemies' (verso blank). F2 text. H1 title of 'Of the Diseases of the Mind and the Body ... by Plutarchus Chaeronensis' (verso blank). H2 text. H6 title of 'Of the Diseases of the Mind, and the Body ... by Maximus Tirius' (verso blank). H7 text. I6ᵛ blank. I7 title of 'The Praise and Happinesse of the Countrie-Life' (verso blank). I8 text. χ1 errata (verso blank).

Catchwords: B–C, With   D–E, That   F–G, happily [happily,]   I–K, and K–L, the

RT (A4/5) The Epistle/Dedicatory. (A5ᵛ) The Epistle, &c. (A6ᵛ) The Publisher to the Reader. (B1ᵛ–E8ᵛ) Olor Iscanus.

BM (238.b.41)–χ1, L8, wants A1. Bodl. (8⁰ M5 Art. BS) + χ1, –L8; (Antiq. f. E4/1)–χ1, L8. ULC, + χ1, –L8.

Wing V. 123 (+). Martin 3.

[6] [A reissue, with a cancel title, and with the following leaves removed: A1, 2 ('Ad Posteros' and the engraved title) and F1, H1, H6, J7 (the titles of the translations.] Printed, and are to be sold by Peter Parker, 1679.

NLW.
Not in Wing. Martin 10 (listing also Cardiff Public Library).   [Plate 6]

Paulinus, of Nola (Translation from)

See no. 2.

Poems

Secular poems. With a translation of Juvenal's tenth satire into English verse. Entered in SR 15 September 1646.

[7] Poems, with the tenth satyre of Juvenal Englished. *For G. Badger*,
1646. **[Plate 7]**

8⁰. §⁴ A–E⁸ F⁴ (§1, A1 blank.). Paginated (A2) 3–87.

§2 title (verso blank). §3 To all Ingenious Lovers of Poesie', signed: H.V.'
A2 text, with HP and initial. C7 title of 'Iuvenals tenth satyre translated'
(verso blank). C8 text. F4ᵛ blank.

Catchwords: A–B, To   C–D, He [He,]   E4–5, Ca- [Catarrhs,]   E–F, But

RT (§3/4) To all Ingenious/Lovers of Pooesie. (§4ᵛ) To all Ingenious Lovers, &c.

BM (C.56.b.16)–§1, A1; (E.1178/3)–§1, A1; (1077.c.6/1) imp. A2–C6 only.

Worcester College, Oxford, + §1, A1 (folded round to front of §).

Wing V. 124 (+) Martin 1

Praise and Happiness of the Countrie-Life

See nos. 5, 6.

Silex Scintillans

*Religious poems. Entered in SR 28 March 1650; re-entered 20 March
1654/5.*

[8] Silex scintillans: or sacred poems and private ejaculations.
T.W. for H. Blunden, 1650. **[Plate 8]**

Printer: Thomas Walkley.

8⁰. A–G⁸ (G8 blank). Paginated (A4ᵛ) 8–110 (misprinting 67 as 97).

A1 blank. A1ᵛ 'Authoris (de se) Emblema', 16 ll. verse. A2 title, engraved
(verso blank). A3 The Dedication', 14 ll. verse (verso blank). A4 text, with
HT, lace ornament and initial.

Catchwords: A–B, The   B–C, *Vanity* [Vanity]   E–F, Nothing   F–G, So

RT (A4/5–G6/7) *Silex Scintillans/Or Sacred Poems.* (G7ᵛ) *Silex Scintillans*

BM (238.b.8). Bodl. (Don.f208) – G8 (A2 bound before A1). Worcester College,
Oxford, +G8, wants G3–6.

Wing V. 125 (+) Martin 2 (listing also NLW.)

[9] Silex scintillans: sacred poems and private ejaculations. The
second edition. *For Henry Crips, and Lodowick Lloyd*, 1655.

[Plate 9]

A reissue of the sheets of the 1650 edition, with a new title and some new
preliminaries, two cancel leaves in the text, and a second part not previously
printed.

8⁰. A⁸ (–A1–3 + ᵖA⁴B⁸) B⁸ (± B2, 3) C–G⁸ ²C–G⁸ H⁴. (ᵖA1 blank? G8
blank.) Paginated (A4ᵛ) 8–110 (misprinting 67 as 97). (²C1) 1–84 (misprinting 80 as 90).

πA2 title, printed (verso blank). πA3 'The Authors Preface to the following Hymns', dated Newton by Usk, near Skethrock, Septem.30.1654'. πB4ᵛ blank. πB5 Begin 'O Lord, the hope of Israel'. πB6ᵛ 'To my most merciful . . . Redeemer', in verse. πB8ᵛ verse beginning 'Vain Wits and eyes . . .' A4 text of 'Silex Scintillans' with HT, lace ornament and initial. On G7ᵛ 'Finis'. ²C1 text of second part of 'Silex Scintillans' with HT, lace ornament and initial. H3 table.

Catchwords: πA–B, forbear, πB8–A4, *Silex* [Silex] ²C–D, Trinity [Trinity-Sunday.] ²E–F, And [And] ²G–H, When

RT (πA3ᵛ–B4) *The Preface.* (πB7–8) *The Dedication.* (A4/5–G6/7) *Silex Scintillans/Or Sacred Poems.* (G7ᵛ) *Silex Scintillans* (²C1/2–H1/2) *Silex Scintillans,/Or Sacred Poems.* (²H2ᵛ) *Silex Scintillans, or Sacred Poems.* (²H3ᵛ–H4ᵛ) *The Table.*

BM (C.124.b.26)–πA1, –G8. Bodl. (Arch. A. f. 106)–πA1, +G8.

Wing V. 126 (+) Martin 6 (listing also NLW.).

Thalia Rediviva

Secular poems, including verse translations from Boethius and Claudian. No entry in SR.

[10] Thalia rediviva. The pass-times and diversions of a countrey-muse. *For Robert Pawlet*, 1678. **[Plate 10]**

8⁰. A–G⁸. Paginated (B1) 1–93.

A1 title (verso blank). A2 'To . . . Henry Lord Marquis and Earl of Worcester', signed: J.W.' A4 'To the Reader', signed: 'I.W.' A4ᵛ To Mr. Henry Vaughan . . . upon these and his former Poems' unsigned verses. A5ᵛ Upon the Ingenious Poems of . . . Mr. Henry Vaughan', in verse, signed: Tho. Powel'. A6 'To the ingenious Author', in verse, signed: 'N.W.Jes.Coll.Oxon.' A7 'To . . . Mr. Henry Vaughan', in verse, signed: 'I.W. A.M.Oxon'. A8 text, with HT 'Choice Poems on several occasions', and lace ornament. On B1 HT 'Thalia Rediviva'. F5ᵛ blank. F6 title of 'Eugenii Philalethis . . . Vertumnus et Cynthia' (verso blank). F7 'Ornatissimo viro . . . Mathaeo Herbert', in verse, signed 'E.P.' F7ᵛ text. G7ᵛ 'A Catalogue of Books Printed for, and sold by Robert Pawlet.

Catchwords: A–B, *Thalia* C–D, Though E–F, Thou F–G, *Appia*

RT (A2ᵛ–A3ᵛ) *The Epistle Dedicatory.* (A8ᵛ) *Choice Poems,* &c. (B1/2–G6/7) *Choice Poems/On several Occasions.* (G8–G8ᵛ) *A Catalogue of Books.*

BM (C.39.b.33). Bodl. (Antiq. f. E4/1).

Wing V. 127 (+) Martin 9.

41

MARVELL

MARVELL, Andrew (1621-1678)

Born near Hull and educated at Hull Grammar School and Trinity College Cambridge. Travelled on the continent. In 1650 he became tutor to the daughter of Lord Fairfax at Nun Appleton, Yorkshire. There he wrote some of his best-known poems in praise of gardens and the country life. In 1653 he became tutor to Cromwell's ward, William Dutton, and in 1657 Milton's assistant as Latin Secretary to the Council. Wrote several poems in Cromwell's honour. After the Restoration he entered Parliament and wrote satires and pamphlets attacking the corruption of ministers, the policy of alliance with France and the growth of 'Popery' in the England of Charles II. Much of his prose is in defence of the Nonconformists against the intolerance of the Anglican Establishment.

Chronology of the Publication of Marvell's works to 1700

[1648.] *An Elegy upon the Death of my Lord Francis Villiers.* An anonymous poem, probably by Marvell.

1655. *The First Anniversary of the Government under his Highness the Lord Protector.* An anonymous poem. Reprinted in *Miscellaneous Poems,* 1681.

1665. *The Character of Holland.* An anonymous poem. Written in 1653, now printed for the first time, in a truncated version and with additions by another hand. Reprinted in 1672. The full text was printed in *Miscellaneous Poems,* 1681.

1672. *The Character of Holland.* First published 1665.

The Rehearsal Transpros'd. A prose satire against Samuel Parker and in defence of the Nonconformists. Three editions in this year, all anonymous and all bearing a fictitious imprint. Two are known to have been printed at London for Nathaniel Ponder; the third is a pirated edition.

1673. Another edition of the preceding, likewise anonymous and bearing a fictitious imprint but probably printed at London.

The Rehearsall Transpros'd: the second part. A prose satire, answering Parker's reply to *The Rehearsal Transpros'd.* It bears Marvell's name and also the name of the publisher: Nathaniel Ponder of London.

1674. Another edition of the preceding, with Ponder's imprint.

1676.   *Mr. Smirke; or, the Divine in Mode.* A prose satire against
          Francis Turner and in defence of the Nonconformists. Written
          under the pseudonym: 'Andreas Rivetus Junior'. Together
          with 'A Short Historical Essay touching General Councils',
          an appeal to early church history to undermine the Anglican
          position against the Nonconformists. Two editions, both
          without imprint.

1677 [1677/78] *An Account of the Growth of Popery, and Arbitrary Govern-
          ment in England.* A prose tract attacking the government and
          the French alliance. Anonymous, and bearing a false
          Amsterdam imprint. Printed at London.

[1678]   Another edition of the preceding, undated but evidently
          printed after his death (16 August 1678) as it bears his
          name on the titlepage. With a false Amsterdam imprint.
          Printed at London.

1678.   *Remarks upon a Late Disingenuous Discourse.* A prose satire
          against Thomas Danson, the Calvinist. Anonymous.

1680.   French translation of *An Account of the Growth of Popery.*
          Translator unknown. With a false Hamburg imprint.

          A Short Historical Essay touching General Councils. Previously
          printed with *Mr. Smirke*, 1676, now printed separately for
          the first time.

1681.   *Miscellaneous Poems.* Some previously printed but many others
          here appearing in print for the first time.

          Another edition of *Mr. Smirke* (first printed 1676).

1687.   Another edition of *A Short Historical Essay* (first printed
          separately 1680).

1689.   *Mr. Andrew Marvell's Character of Popery,* an extract from *An
          Account of the Growth of Popery* (first printed 1677/8). With
          an introduction by an anonymous editor.

Account of the Growth of Popery

*A prose tract attacking the government and the French alliance. Written
late in 1677 and published early in 1688, it deals with the period 1675
to the end of 1677, accusing the government of suppressing parliament and
the Protestant religion and favouring political and religious tyranny. The
first edition was anonymous. It was answered by Sir Roger L'Estrange ('An
Account of the Growth of Knavery', 1678) who plainly hints that Marvell
was the author. The second edition, published a few months after Marvell's
death, which occurred on 16 August 1678, bears his name on the titlepage.*

A French translation, presumably aimed at enlisting Huguenot sympathy for the Whig cause at the time of the Exclusion crisis, was published in 1680. An extract from the original English version, entitled 'Mr. Andrew Marvell's Character of Popery', was published after the Revolution, both separately (in 1689) and as part of State Tracts (1689 and 1693). Wing lists an edition of the original tract (M.862, Chetham's Library only) with date 1678 in the imprint, but this is a 'ghost'. No entry in SR.

[1] An account of the growth of Popery, and arbitrary government in England. *Amsterdam*, 1677 [1677/8].　　　　　　　**[Plate 1]**

Anon. Imprint false; printed at London?

4⁰. A–T⁴ U². ²A–L². Paginated (A2) 3–156 (misprinting 56 as 65, 122 as 119 127 as 108). (²A2) 3–44.

A1 title (verso blank). A2 text, with HT and plain initial in frame of lace ornament. On U2ᵛ errata. ²A1 title of A List of Several Ships' (verso blank). ²A2 text, beginning 'At the Court at White-Hall'

Catchwords: A–B, and D–E, (Mer-)chant [Men] H–I, there [there,] L–M, The [*An*] T–U, (Vali-)dity

No RT.

Bodl. (G Pamph, 1120/5). ULC. The following copies all want ²A–L: BM (702.e.4/2); (C.55.d.20/1); (Ashley 1104). Bodl. (Pamph. C. 138/12); (G. Pamph. 1359/22); (Ashm. 733/3*a*).

Wing M. 860 (+)

[2] [Another edition.] *Amsterdam* [1678].　　　　　　　　**[Plate 2]**

Posthumous. With 'By Andrew Marvel' on the titlepage. Printed at London? Fol. A–S². Paginated (A2) 3–68 (repeating 5–8).

A1 title (verso blank). A2 text, with lace ornament and HT. P2 title of 'A list of several ships belonging to English Merchants taken by French privateers' (verso blank). Q1 'At the Court at White-Hall . . .' R1 the list. On S1ᵛ 'An additional list of ships'. On S2 'A Continuation of a List of Ships'. On S2ᵛ 'A List of other Ships taken'.

Catchwords: A–B, which F–G, Forces [Forces,] N–O, *Doubtless* R–S, *June*

No RT.

BM (4707.h.12); (T.88*/11) cropped. Bodl. (C11.15Th). TCD.

Wing M. 861 (+)

[3] Relation de l'accroissement de la Papauté et du gouvernement absolu en Angleterre. *Hambourgh, Pierre Pladt*, 1680.　　**[Plate 3]**

Translator unknown. Imprint false; printed in France? The appendix entitled 'Proces de Mr. Harrington' is fuller than in the English editions'. 12⁰. A–K¹² L⁶ (L6 blank). Paginated (A2) 3–245.

A1 title (verso blank) A2 text, with HT and initial. K8 'Proces de Mr. Harrington a l'occasion de ces troubles'.

Catchwords: A–B, Qui, [Quiconque] E–F, (cri-)me, I–H, (se-)rieu- [rieusement] K–L, Har- [Harrington;]
No RT.

Bodl. (Vet.D3 f.79) + L6. ULC

[4] Mr. Andrew Marvell's character of Popery. *For Richard Baldwin,* 1689. **[Plate 4]**

An extract from *An Account of the Growth of Popery*, with an anonymous introduction praising the constitution of the Church of England.

4⁰. A⁴. Paginated (A2) 3–8.

A1 title (verso blank). A2 text, with HT.

Catchwords: A2–3, once A3–4, Warrs,

No RT.

BM (3935.dd.2); (3935.cc.30); (3935.d.15). Bodl. (Pamph. 196/8.)
Wing M. 866 (+)

Advice to a Painter

This verse satire against James Duke of York, originally published as a separate tract with no author's name, has been shown by Margoliouth to be the work of Henry Savile. Wing misdates it [1666]; the date should be [1673]. The misattribution to Marvell appears to date from its republication in 'State Poems', 1689, eleven years after Marvell's death. Not included in the present catalogue.

Character of Holland

A verse satire. Written in 1653 during the First Dutch War but not, apparently, printed at the time. The first appearance of the full text in print was in 'Miscellaneous Poems', 1681. A truncated version, without Marvell's name and with additions apparently by another hand, was printed in 1665 during the Second Dutch War, and again in 1672 during the Third Dutch War. Entered in SR 13 June 1665.

[5] [Head-title:] The character of Holland. [Colophon:] *T. Mabb for Robert Horn,* 1665. **[Plates 5, 6]**

Anon.

Fol. A–B². Paginated (A1) 1–7.

A1 text, with HT and initial. On B1 *FINIS*. and colophon.

Catchwords: A1–2, A A–B, Sure B1–2, Vainly

No RT

Hunt.

Wing M. 867 (citing this copy only).

[6] The character of Holland. *For Rob. Horn*, 1672.   [**Plate 7**]

Anon.

4⁰. A⁴. Paginated (A2) 1–5.

A1 title (verso blank). A2 text, with HT, HP and initial. A4ᵛ blank.

Catchwords: A2–3, Among   A3–4, They

No RT.

BM (C.71.h.13).

Wing M. 868 (+)

Character of Popery

See no. 4.

Common-Place Book out of the Rehearsal Transprosed

Wing (M.869) treats this as if it were a work by Marvell, whereas it is really an anonymous reply to Marvell's 'The Rehearsal Transpros'd'.

Elegy upon the Death of My Lord Francis Villiers

A poem printed without name of author or date. The attribution to Marvell is based on a MS note by George Clarke (1660–1736) on the copy that he left to Worcester College, Oxford. Margoliouth is inclined to accept the attribution (see pp. 332–3 for a discussion both of the poem and of the reliability of Clarke as a witness). The date can be determined by the subject matter: Lord Francis Villiers, the posthumous son of the first Duke of Buckingham, was killed in a skirmish near Kingston-on-Thames on 7 July 1648. No entry in SR.

[7] An elegy upon the death of my lord Francis Villiers. [*n.p.*, 1648.]
                                                              [**Plate 8**]

Anon.

4⁰. A⁴. Paginated (A2) 3–8.

A1 title (verso blank). A2 text with HT.

Catchwords: A2–3, Made   A3–4, Th'

No RT.

Worcester College, Oxford.

Wing M. 870 (listing this copy only).

First Anniversary of the Government under his Highness the Lord Protector

A poem. Published separately in 1655; reprinted in 'Miscellaneous Poems', 1681. No entry in SR.

[8] The first anniversary of the government under his highness the Lord Protector. *By Thomas Newcomb; sold by Samuel Gellibrand,* 1655. **[Plate 9]**

Anon.

4⁰. A–C⁴. Paginated (A2) 1–21.

A1 title (verso blank). A2 text, with HT 'The Anniversary', HP and initial. C4ᵛ blank.

Catchwords: A–B, But   B–C, The   B3–4, *B*ut [But]

No RT.

BM (E.480/1). Bodl. (X47 Jur/18) wanting C4.

Wing M. 871 (+)

History of the Twelve Caesars

A 17th century manuscript note on one of the Bodleian copies (Art. 8⁰ʃ 43) of this translation of Suetonius, published in 1672, ascribes the translation to Marvell. But, as Legouis points out (Legouis, p. 467), there are two considerations that should make us hesitate to accept the ascription without further evidence: (1.) The translation is of a very pedestrian quality for a writer of Marvell's stature; (2.) When Marvell cites passages from Suetonius in translation in the second part of 'The Rehearsall Transpros'd', 1673, the version he uses is not identical with that in the 'History of the Twelve Caesars'. Not included in the present catalogue.

Miscellaneous Poems

Some previously printed but many others here appearing in print for the first time. Published three years after the author's death with a prefatory note signed 'Mary Marvell' [Mary Palmer, his housekeeper], attesting their authenticity. As first printed (no. 9 below) the collection included the three long poems in honour of Cromwell: 'An Horatian Ode upon Cromwel's Return from Ireland', 'The First Anniversary of the Government under O.C.' and 'A Poem upon the Death of O.C.' At some stage in publication it was decided to suppress these three poems and the leaves containing them were cancelled (no. 9a below). See Margoliouth pp. 206–7. Facsimile reprint of the text in its original state (BM C.59.i.8) together with MS. additions to the later state (Bodl. MS. Eng. Poet. d. 49) by the Scolar Press, Menston, 1969.

[9] Miscellaneous poems. *For Robert Boulter*, 1681.   [**Plate 10**]

fol. π1 A² B–C² D–U⁴ [X²]. Paginated (B1) 1–14[6].

π1 engraved portrait (verso blank). A1 title (verso blank). A2 'To the Reader', signed: 'Mary Marvell' attesting the authenticity of the poems (verso blank). B1 text.

Catchwords: B–C, And   D–E, The   F–G, VI.   H–I, While   L–M, *Upon*   Q–R, Hence   S–T, 'Needs   T–U, *Cynthia*.

RT *Miscellanies*.

BM (C.59.i.8.) wanting X1, 2. Hunt., wanting T2–X2. In the BM copy there is an unexplained stub between R3 and R4. As the volume has been tightly rebound it is not at present possible to see whether the stub is conjugate with R1; if it is, this copy is probably a curiosity, R2–X2 having first been cut away in order to permit of the alterations noted above, and then a set of the same leaves unaltered having been bound in their place.

Wing M. 872 (+ Not distinguished from no. 9a).

[9a] R2–T1 and U2–X2, comprising for the most part three long poems on Cromwell, have been cancelled and replaced by single leaves, signed S1 and X1, which bridge the gap by reprinting the non Cromwellian parts of the cancelled leaves.

                                                              [**No Plate**]

BM (G.2449/2); Ashley 4898. Bodl. (Ashmole 1094/6) wanting π1; (G Pamph. 2204/62) wanting π1; (MS.Eng.Poet.d 49) wanting A2, G2–3, P4, Q1–3, S1, but with the missing poems (including the Cromwell poems from the cancellanda) added in contemporary manuscript. Worcester College, Oxford.

Wing M. 872 (not distinguished from no. 9).

Mr. Smirke; or, the Divine in Mode

A prose satire directed at Francis Turner, Master of St. John's College, Cambridge, who had attacked the Nonconformists in a work entitled 'Animadversions upon . . . the Naked Truth'. The title is taken from a minor character in Etherage's 'Man of Mode'. Marvell's work, published under

51

the pseudonym 'Andreas Rivetus Junior', is a powerful plea for toleration for the Nonconformists. Tacked on to it is another, anonymous, work by him: 'A Short Historical Essay, touching General Councils', an appeal to early church history to undermine the Anglican position against the Nonconformists. 'A Short Historical Essay', was later published separately (see nos. 19, 20). Wing lists an edition of 'Mr. Smirke' with date 1681 in the imprint (Wing M.874, TCD only), but this is a 'ghost'. A bibliographical study by Miss M. Pollard, based on the copies at Trinity College, Dublin, is to appear in a future issue of 'Long Room; published by the friends of the Library'. No entry in SR.

[**10**] Mr. Smirke; or, the divine in mode . . . By Andreas Rivetus, Junior, [n.p.], 1676. [**Plate 11**]

Anon.

4°. A1 χ1 B–F⁴ g⁴ (–g4) G-I⁴ ²I⁴ K⁴. Paginated (B1) 1–76 (leaving 6 pages unnumbered between 40 and 41, and repeating 61–4, with 61 and 62 in reverse order; and misnumbering 56 as 43).

A1 title (verso blank). χ1 'To the Captious Reader'. B1 text, with HT.

Catchwords: χ1–χ1ᵛ, more B–C, tending F–g, by H1–2, most H2–3, (Prin-)cipality, H3–4, these I-²I, (usur-)pin₃ [ping] ²I–K, necessary[necessary,]

No RT.

In this edition, χ1 has 20 lines of text; p. 76 has 21 lines of text and FINIS in italic capitals (not swash).

Bodl. (Ashm.1231/4); (Firth e 8/11) wanting title. TCD (P.gg.21/3). The following have the title of no. 10a (Plate 12): BM (701.g.10/14. ULC (Bb.9.7/10); (G.10.33/5).

Wing M. 873 (+ Not distinguished from 10a and 11).

[**10a**] [A variant state.] [**Plate 12**]

Made up from sheets of no. 10 except for: (1.) the title, which is of a different setting; (2.) gatherings F and H. The inner forme of F is printed from the same setting as no. 10, the outer forme is substantially different. The inner forme of H is printed from the same setting as no. 11 the outer forme is substantially different.

Page 56 is correctly numbered.

Catchwords of gathering H: H1–2, generally H2–3, (Princi-)pality, H3–4, aside.

TCD (GG.n.30/4). Bodl. (Pamph.c.136/12) with title of no 10. (Plate 11) Wing M. 873 (not distinguished from 10 and 11).

[11] [Another edition.] [*n.p.*], 1676.   [**Plate 13**]

Anon.

Collation as in no. 10, but in the repeated run of pp. 61–4, 61 and 62 are in correct order. Contents as in no. 10.

Catchwords: χ1– χ1^v, better B–C, tending [intending] F–g, by H1–2 generally H2–3, *Bishops* H3–4, *aside*, H–I, some I–^{2}I, usurping [ping] ^{2}I–K, *necessary*

No RT.̇

In this edition, misprints in 'To the Captious Reader' are corrected; χ1 has 18 lines of text; p. 76 has 23 lines of text and *FINIS* in swash capitals.

Bodl. (D 12 1 Linc/4); (G Pamh 1052/5)wants A1, χ1. TCD. (LL.o.14/6).

Wing. M. 873 (not distinguished from 10 and 10a).

Plain Dealing

The work entitled 'Plain dealing: or, a Full and Particular Examination of a Late Treatise entituled, Humane Reason . . . By A.M. a Countrey Gentleman' is attributed to Marvell in the British Museum Catalogue presumably on the strength of the initials 'A.M.' There appears to be no evidence to support the attribution and, as Legouis points out, both the matter (it is a plea for firm authority in the Church of England) and the style are against it. Not included in the present catalogue.

Rehearsal Transpros'd

A prose satire against Samuel Parker (afterwards Bishop of Oxford), the author of 'A Discourse of Ecclesiastical Policy' and other anti-Non-Conformist writings, including a preface to Bishop Bramhall's 'Vindication', 1672. The title is taken from Buckingham's satire 'The Rehearsal'. All editions are anonymous. After the appearance of the first issue attempts were made by the censor to suppress the work, but the King, whose policy of toleration for Nonconformists the author praises, intervened to save it. Some alterations insisted on by the censor were incorporated in the second edition (see no. 14). Modern edition: 'The Rehearsal Transpros'd and The Rehearsal Transps'd. The second part. Edited by D.I.B. Smith.', Oxford, 1971. No entry in SR.

[12] The rehearsal transpros'd: or, animadversions upon a late book. *London, A.B. for the assigns of John Calvin and Theodore Beza, at the sign of the Kings Indulgence, on the south side of the Lake Lemane,* 1672.

[Plate 14]

Anon. Printer: Anne Brewster? for Nathaniel Ponder. (cf. Smith p. xxi).
8⁰. A^2 B–X^8 Y^4 (A1, Y4 blank?). Paginated (B1) 1–326 (misprinting 190 as 191, 191 as 192).

A2 title (verso blank). B1 text, with lace ornament and HT 'Animadversions upon the Preface to Bishop Bramhall's Vindication'. On $Y3^v$ errata.

Catchwords: B–C, yet   G–H, (Prefer-)ment, [ment]   M–N, (re-)verencing ["verencing]   X–Y, knows

No RT.

BM (C.131.b.22)–A1, Y4. ULC,–A1, Y4.

Wing M.878. (+ Not distinguished from 12a and 12b) Smith records a variant with 'Leman' in the imprint (Harvard and Chapin).

[12a] [With a cancel title.] *London,* 1672.   **[Plate 15]**

Oxford English Faculty Library.

[12b] [A variant cancel title.]   **[Plate 16]**

BM (uncatalogued)–A1, Y4. Bodl. (8°C118.Linc.)–A1, Y4.

[13] The second edition, corrected. *London, A.B. for the assings* [*sic*] *of John Calvin and Theodore Beza, at the sign of the Kings Indulgence, on the south-side of the Lake Lemane, 1672.*   **[Plate 17]**

Anon. A pirated edition.

12⁰. A^2 B–H^{12} I^6 K^2 (A1 blank? misprinting D4 as D3). Paginated (B1) 1–181 (repeating 71–2, transposing 140 and 141, misprinting 153 as 134, 160 as 164, 164 as 160, 165 as 153).

A2 title (verso blank). B1 text, with HT 'Animadversions upon the Preface to Bishop Bramhall's Vindication'. $K2^v$ blank.

Catchwords: B–C, if   G–H, *aliquid*, [*aliquid.*]   I–K, how

No RT.

This edition derives textually from the first edition (cf. Smith p. xxv) and incorporates the 'errata', but it introduces many new errors, (cf. note to no. 14 below).

BM (4103.a.28)–A1 Bodl. (Vet. A3 f.755) + A1?

Not in Wing.

[14] The second impression, with additions and amendments. *London, J.D. for the assigns of John Calvin and Theodore Beza, at the sign of the King's Indulgence, on the south-side the Lake Lemane; sold by N. Ponder,* 1672. **[Plate 18]**

Anon. Printed: John Darby for Nathaniel Ponder. (cf. Smith p. xxiii)

8⁰. *A*² B–X⁸ Y⁴ (A1 Y4 blank). Paginated (B1) 1–326 (correcting the misprints of the first edition but misprinting 230–31 as 214, 219, and 265 as 165).

*A*2 title. *A*2ᵛ 'An Advertisement from the Bookseller', signed: 'N.P.' B1 text, with lace ornament and HT 'Animadversions upon the Preface to Bishop Bramhall's Vindication'.

Catchwords as in no. 12, except: (BM copy) M–N, *them*-["themselves] First 2 lines on N1 in roman. Both ULC copies have: *them*-[*themselves*] and first 2 lines on N1 in italic.

No RT.

A fairly close reprint of the first edition, incorporating some changes and omissions insisted on by the censor (cf. Smith p. xxiii) and also some stylistic alterations and additions. The corrections called for in the errata list of the first edition have, with one or two exceptions, been made. The bookseller in his Advertisement (A2ᵛ) complains about the publication of a pirated edition: 'This book having wrought it self thorow many difficulties, it hath newly incountred with that of a counterfeit impression in 12⁰ under the title and pretence of the 2d Edition corrected. Whereas in truth that impression is so far from having been corrected that it doth grossly and frequently corrupt both the sence and words of the coppy'.

BM (1019.e.12)–A1, Y4; (G.19514)–A1, Y4. Bodl. (Vet. A3 f 531) + Y4, ?A1. ULC + A1, Y4.

Wing M.879 (+ Not distinguished from 14a).

[14a] [A variant, titlepage.] **[Plate 19]**

BM (1485.k.17) + A1, Y4. Bodl. (Vet. A3 f 628); (Ashm. 1591).

[15] [Another edition.] *London, J.X. for the Assigns of John Calvin and Theodore Beza, at the sign of the King's Indulgence, on the south-side the Lake-Lemane,* 1673. **[Plate 20]**

Anon. A pirated edition, set up by two or more compositors working independently (Smith p. xxx).

12⁰. A–B¹² D–G¹² ²G¹² H¹² K–L¹² ²L¹² M–N¹² O⁶. Paginated (A2) 1–322 (omitting 47–8, 191–2, 301–10; repeating 143–4, 229–40; misprinting 97 as 65, 209 as 219, 314 as 114, 319 as 119).

A1 title (verso blank). A2 text, headed 'Animadversions upon the Preface to Bishop Bramhall's Vindication, &c.' On O6ᵛ *FINIS.*

Catchwords: A–B, have   B–D, still   G–²G, (a-) sham'd [shamed]   H–K, he
L–²L, but   N–O, first

No RT.

University of Leicester.

Wing M.881a (listing only the American Antiquarian Society copy).

Rehearsal Transpros'd. Part 2

Answering Parker's 'A Reproof to the Rehearsal Transprosed', *1673.*

[**16**]   The rehearsall transpros'd: the second part. *For Nathaniel Ponder*,
1673.   [**Plate 21**]

8⁰. π² A–Z⁸ 2A–2C⁸ (±E5, 6; most copies ± I2; 2C8 blank). Paginated
(A1)1–414. (misprinting 66 as 56, 135 as 125, 320 as 292).

π1 blank. π1ᵛ 'Reproof p. 67. If you have any thing to object . . .' π2 title
(verso blank). A1 text, with HT. On 2C7ᵛ errata.

Catchwords: A–B, sake   G–H, out,   O–P, Espe-[Especially]   V–X, from
2B–2C, make

No RT.

BM (1019.e.13) + 2C8; (G.19515)–2C8. Bodl. (8.C558 Linc.) ULC (1)
+ 2C8; (2) + 2C8; (3)–2C8. Christ Church, Oxford. Dr. Williams's Library.
In all copies examined E5, 6 are cancels. In the Bodley copy and both the BM
copies I2 is a cancel introducing a textual correction in which words previously
put into the mouth of Tomkins, Parker's fellow-chaplain, are attributed to his
examining professor.

Wing M.882 (+)

[**17**]   [Another edition.] *For Nathaniel Ponder*, 1674.   [**Plate 22**]

12⁰. π² A–P¹² Q⁶ (misprinting G3 as G5). Paginated (A1)1–372 (misprinting
201–2 as 221–2; 258–62 as 358–62).
π1 blank. π1ᵛ 'Reproof. p. 67 . . . [as before]' π2 title (verso blank). A1 text,
with HT and lace ornament.
Catchwords: A–B, he   G–H, manner   O–P, but   P–Q, *indeed*
No RT.
BM (1607/3406). Bodl. (Vet A3 f.399). Christ Church, Oxford. Worcester
College, Oxford. ULC.
Wing M.883 (+)

Relation de l'Accroissement de la Papauté

See no. 3.

Remarks upon a Late Disingenuous Discourse

A prose satire attacking Thomas Danson, the Calvinist, and the doctrine of Predestination maintained in his 'De Causa Dei', 1678. No entry in SR.

[**18**] Remarks upon a late disingenuous discourse. *Printed and are to be sold by Christopher Hussey,* 1678. **[Plate 23]**

Anon. Titlepage: 'By a Protestant'.

8⁰. π^2 A–K⁸ (K7, 8 blank). Paginated (A1) 1–155 (misprinting 32 as 33, 50 as 52).

π1 blank. π1ᵛ 'Imprimatur, Apr. 17. 1678'. π2 title (verso blank). A1 text, with HT. K6ᵛ errata.

Catchwords: A–B, both D–E, Distin- [Distinctions,] F–G, The H–I, (*Sen-*)*ses*,

No RT.

BM (480.a.18)–K7, 8, wanting π1. Bodl. (8⁰ N 93 Th.) + K7 and stub of K8. Wing M.884.

Seasonable Argument to Persuade all the Grand Juries of England

This prose tract, printed in 1677, has sometimes been attributed to Marvell on the grounds that it is of the same tendency and appeared at the same time as 'An Account of the Growth of Popery'. L'Estrange, in 'An Account of the Growth of Knavery', 1678, insinuates that the two works were by the same author. There appears to be no solid evidence, however, either external or internal, in favour of the attribution. Grosart rejects it; so does Legouis (though less categorically). For a discussion of the matter see Legouise p. 469. Not included in the present catalogue.

Seasonable Question and an Usefull Answer

This prose tract, printed in 1676 and sometimes attributed to Marvell, is almost certainly not by him. There appears to be no external evidence for the attribution and, as Grosart points out, 'the entire composition is legal and has no single characteristic of Marvel'. Rejected by Legouis. Not included in the present catalogue.

ANDREW MARVELL

Second Advice to the Painter

This anonymous political satire, written in 1667, is sometimes attributed to Marvell, but Margoliouth rejects the attribution on internal evidence. His judgment is endorsed by Legouis (in Margoliouth, 3rd ed., pp. 349–50). Not included in the present catalogue.

Short historical Essay touching General Councils

Prose. An appeal to early church history to undermine the Anglican position against the Nonconformists. First printed with 'Mr. Smirke' (see nos. 10–11). No entry in SR.

[**19**] A short historical essay touching general councils. *London*, 1680.
[**Plate 24**]

Anon.

4⁰. A–E⁴ (E4 blank). Paginated (A2) 3–38.

A1 title (verso blank). A2 text, with HT.

Catchwords: A–B, (de-)plores   C–D, (re-)proach   D–E, of

No RT.

In this edition E3ᵛ (p. 38) has 33 lines of text.

BM (702.e.3/14)–E4. Bodl. (G Pamph. 1783/21) + E4; (Ashm. 1231/6) + E4. ULC.

Wing M.888 (+)

[**20**] [Another edition.] *For R. Baldwin*, 1687.
[**Plate 25**]

Anon.

Collation, contents and catchwords as before. E3ᵛ (p. 38) has 26 lines of text, omitting the passage beginning: 'And particularly that the Arch-deacon of Canterbury being in ill humor upon account of his Ecclesiastical Policy, may not revenge himself upon the innocent Walloons . . .'

BM (T.692/30) + E4; (698.i.2/4)–E4, cropped. Bodl. (G Pamph. 56/11) + E4; (Pamph. 174/2)–E4; (Firth e 16/8)–E4. ULC.

Wing M.889 (+)

S'too him Bayes

Wing (M.890) treats this as if it were a work by Marvell, whereas it is really an anonymous reply to Marvell's 'The Rehearsal Transpros'd'.

Suetonius, Gaius Suetonius Tranquillus (translation from)

See History of the Twelve Caesars.

Third Part of Advice to the Painter

Excluded from the present catalogue for the same reasons as the 'Second Advice'.

Acknowledgments

I am indebted to the following libraries for permission to reproduce the title-pages of books in their possession:

Bodleian Library, Oxford (Herbert, plates 3, 10, 11, 19, 20, 23, 25. Crashaw, plates 1, 2, 3, 5, 7. Vaughan, plates 2, 5, 10. Marvell, plates 3, 9, 13, 18, 23, 24).

British Museum, London (Herbert, plates 1, 2, 4, 5, 7, 9, 12, 13, 16, 17, 18, 21, 22, 24. Crashaw, plates 6, 8, 9, 10. Vaughan, plates 3, 4, 7, 8, 9. Marvell, plates 1, 2, 4, 7, 10, 12, 14, 16, 17, 19, 21, 22, 25).

Christ Church, Oxford (Vaughan, plate 1).

Henry Huntington Library, California (Crashaw, plate 11, Marvell, plates 5, 6).

Magdalen College, Oxford (Crashaw, plate 4).

National Library of Wales (Vaughan, plate 6).

Oxford English Faculty Library (Marvell, plate 15).

Trinity College, Dublin (Marvell, plate 11).

University Library, Cambridge (Herbert, plates 6, 7, 8).

University of Leicester (Marvell, plate 20).

Worcester College, Oxford (Marvell, plate 8).

ORATIO
Quâ auspicatissimum Serenissimi
PRINCIPIS
CAROLI,
Reditum ex Hispanijs celebrauit
GEORGIVS HERBERT
Academiæ Cantabrigiensis
ORATOR.

Ex Officina CANTRELLI LEGGE, Almæ
Matris Cantabrigiæ *Typographi.*
1623.

HERBERT. PLATE 1 (No. 1).   B.M.(11764.cc.20).

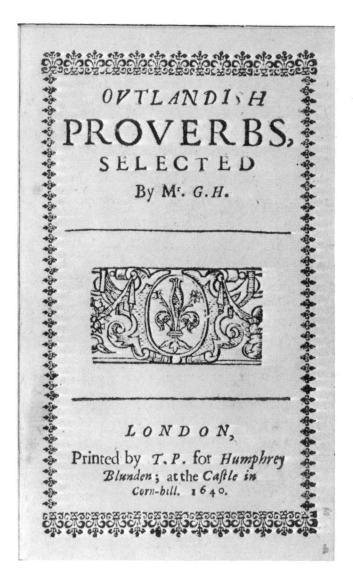

OVTLANDISH
PROVERBS,
SELECTED
By Mr. *G.H.*

LONDON,
Printed by *T.P.* for *Humphrey*
Blunden; at the *Castle in*
Corn-hill. 1640.

HERBERT.   PLATE 2 (No. 2).   B.M.(G.10382).

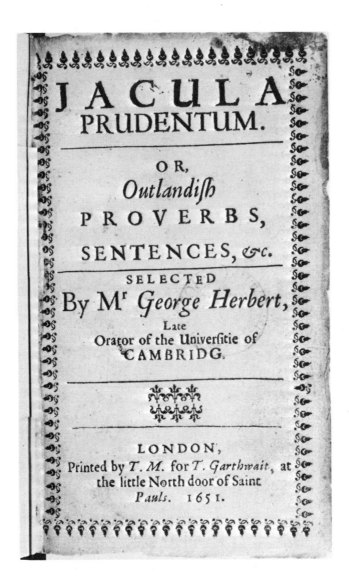

JACULA PRUDENTUM.

OR,
Outlandish
PROVERBS,
SENTENCES, *&c.*

SELECTED

By M*r* *George Herbert*,

Late
Orator of the Univerſitie of
CAMBRIDG.

LONDON,
Printed by *T. M.* for *T. Garthwait*, at
the little North door of Saint
Pauls. 1651.

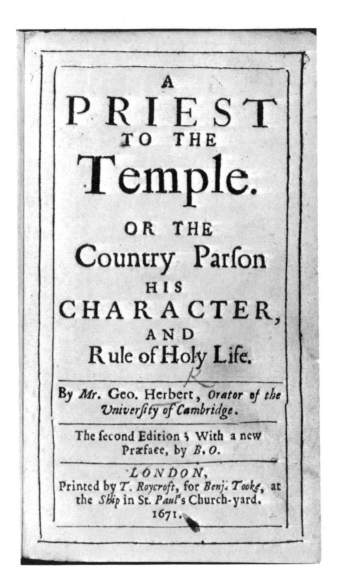

A PRIEST TO THE Temple.

OR THE Country Parson HIS CHARACTER, AND Rule of Holy Life.

By *Mr.* Geo. Herbert, *Orator of the University of Cambridge.*

The second Edition; With a new Præface, by *B. O.*

LONDON,
Printed by *T. Roycroft,* for *Benj. Tooke,* at the *Ship* in St. *Paul's* Church-yard.
1671.

HERBERT. PLATE 4 (No. 4). B.M. (1355.b.9).

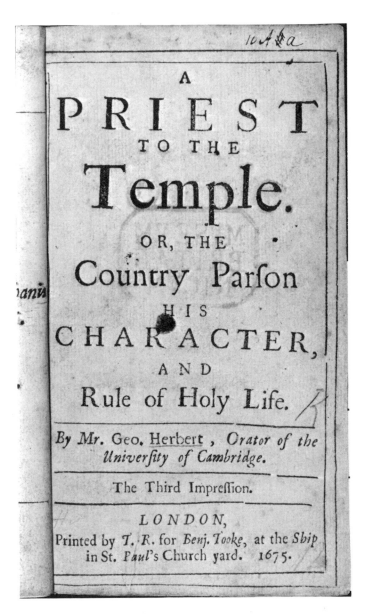

A
PRIEST
TO THE
Temple.

OR, THE
Country Parſon
HIS
CHARACTER,
AND
Rule of Holy Life.

By Mr. Geo. Herbert , *Orator of the University of Cambridge.*

The Third Impreſſion.

LONDON,
Printed by *T. R.* for *Benj. Tooke,* at the *Ship* in St. *Paul*'s Church yard. 1675.

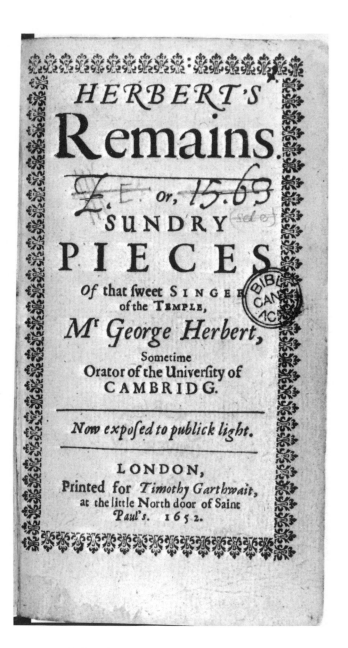

HERBERT'S
Remains.
or,
SUNDRY
PIECES

Of that sweet SINGER
of the TEMPLE,

Mᵣ *George Herbert,*

Sometime
Orator of the Univerſity of
CAMBRIDG.

Now expoſed to publick light.

LONDON,
Printed for *Timothy Garthwaït,*
at the little North door of Saint
Paul's. 1652.

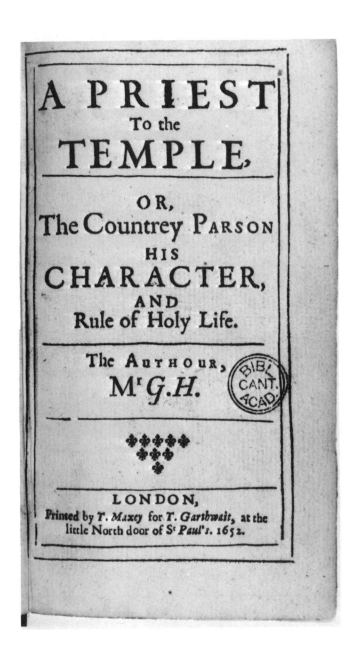

A PRIEST
To the
TEMPLE,
OR,
The Countrey PARSON
HIS
CHARACTER,
AND
Rule of Holy Life.

The AUTHOUR,
Mr *G.H.*

✤✤✤✤✤
✤✤✤
✤

LONDON,
Printed by *T. Maxey* for *T. Garthwait*, at the
little North door of St *Paul's.* 1652.

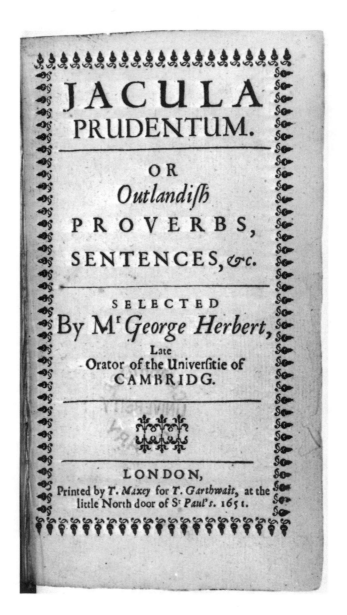

JACULA PRUDENTUM.

OR
Outlandifh
PROVERBS,
SENTENCES, *&c.*

SELECTED
By M.r *George Herbert,*
Late
Orator of the Univerfitie of
CAMBRIDG.

LONDON,
Printed by *T. Maxey* for *T. Garthwait,* at the
little North door of S.t *Paul's.* 1651.

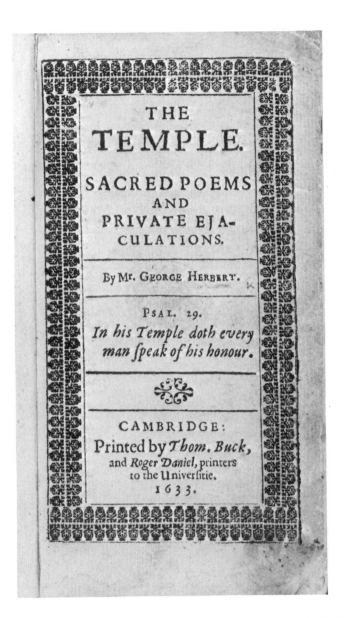

THE
TEMPLE.

SACRED POEMS
AND
PRIVATE EJA-
CULATIONS.

By Mr. GEORGE HERBERT.

PSAL. 29.

In his Temple doth every
man speak of his honour.

CAMBRIDGE:
Printed by *Thom. Buck,*
and *Roger Daniel,* printers
to the Univerſitie.
1 6 3 3.

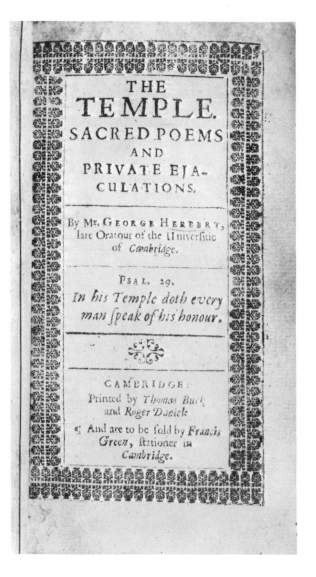

THE
TEMPLE.
SACRED POEMS
AND
PRIVATE EJA-
CULATIONS.

By Mr. GEORGE HERBERT,
late Oratour of the Universitie
of *Cambridge.*

PSAL. 29.

*In his Temple doth every
man speak of his honour.*

CAMBRIDGE:
Printed by *Thomas Buck*
and *Roger Daniel:*

⸿ And are to be sold by *Francis
Green*, stationer in
Cambridge.

HERBERT. PLATE 10 (No. 7a).   Bodl.(Mason.cc.87).

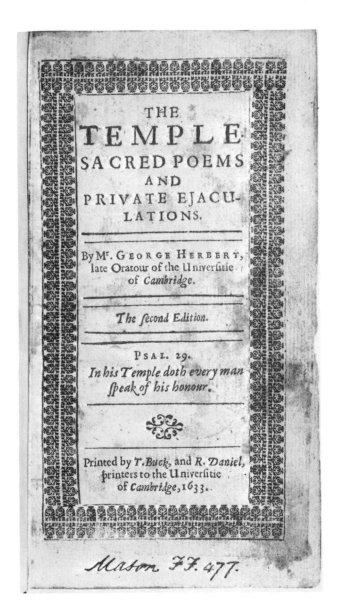

THE
TEMPLE
SACRED POEMS
AND
PRIVATE EJACU-
LATIONS.

By M^r. GEORGE HERBERT,
late Oratour of the Universitie
of *Cambridge.*

The second Edition.

PSAL. 29.
In his Temple doth every man
speak of his honour.

Printed by *T. Buck,* and *R. Daniel,*
printers to the Universitie
of *Cambridge,* 1633.

Mason FF. 477.

HERBERT.   PLATE 12 (No. 8a).   B.M.(1076.i.25).

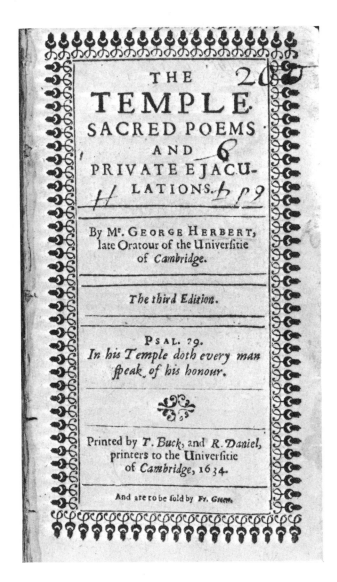

THE 2

TEMPLE.

SACRED POEMS ·

AND 6

PRIVATE EJACU-

LATIONS.

By M꜀. GEORGE HERBERT,
late Oratour of the Universitie
of *Cambridge*.

The third Edition.

PSAL. 29.
*In his Temple doth every man
speak of his honour.*

Printed by *T. Buck*, and *R. Daniel*,
printers to the Universitie
of *Cambridge*, 1634.

And are to be sold by *Fr. Green.*

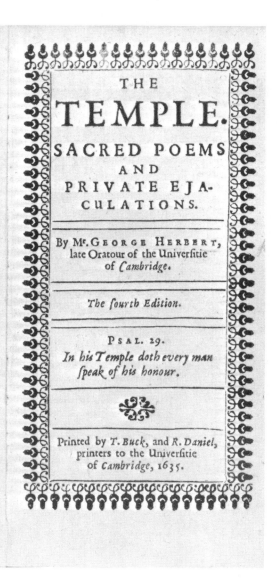

THE
TEMPLE.
SACRED POEMS
AND
PRIVATE EJA-
CULATIONS.

By Mr. GEORGE HERBERT,
late Oratour of the Universitie
of *Cambridge.*

The fourth Edition.

PSAL. 29.
In his Temple doth every man
speak of his honour.

Printed by *T. Buck*, and *R. Daniel*,
printers to the Universitie
of *Cambridge*, 1635.

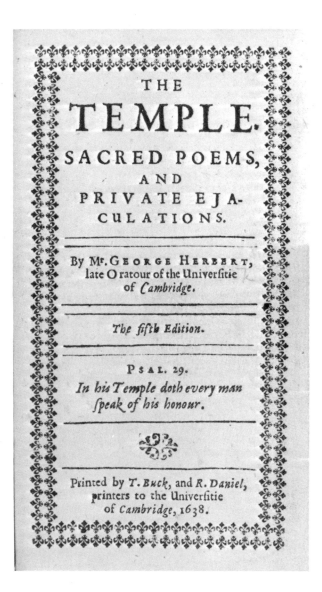

THE
TEMPLE.

SACRED POEMS,
AND
PRIVATE EJA-
CULATIONS.

By Mr. GEORGE HERBERT,
late O ratour of the Univerſitie
of *Cambridge.*

The fifth Edition.

PSAL. 29.

*In his Temple doth every man
ſpeak of his honour.*

Printed by *T. Buck,* and *R. Daniel,*
printers to the Univerſitie
of *Cambridge,* 1638.

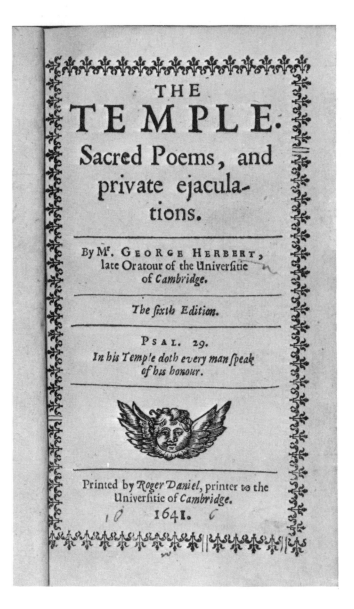

THE
TEMPLE.
Sacred Poems, and private ejacula-tions.

By Mr. GEORGE HERBERT,
late Oratour of the Universitie
of *Cambridge.*

The sixth Edition.

PSAL. 29.
*In his Temple doth every man speak
of his honour.*

Printed by *Roger Daniel*, printer to the
Universitie of *Cambridge.*
1641.

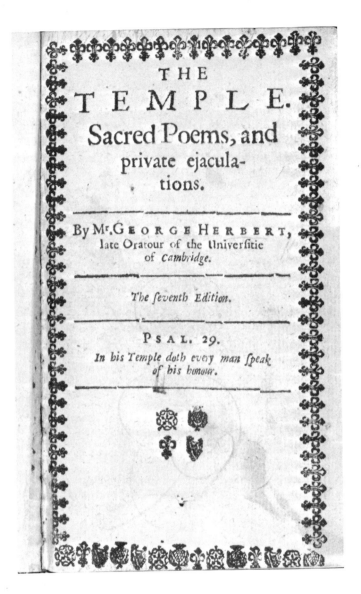

THE
TEMPLE.
Sacred Poems, and
private ejacula-
tions.

By Mr. GEORGE HERBERT,
late Oratour of the Universitie
of *Cambridge*.

The seventh Edition.

PSAL. 29.

In his Temple doth every man speak
of his honour.

HERBERT.   PLATE 17 (No. 13).   B.M.(11626.aa.12).

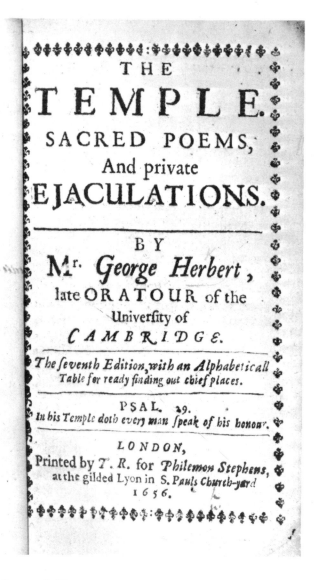

THE
TEMPLE.
SACRED POEMS,
And private
EJACULATIONS.

BY
M^r. *George Herbert,*
late ORATOUR of the
University of
CAMBRIDGE.

The seventh Edition, with an Alphabeticall
Table for ready finding out chief places.

PSAL. 29.
In his Temple doth every man speak of his honour.

LONDON,
Printed by *T. R.* for *Philemon Stephens,*
at the gilded Lyon in S. *Pauls Church-yard*
1 6 5 6.

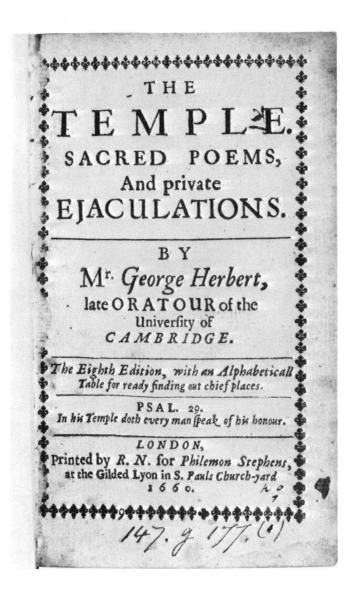

THE

TEMPLE.

SACRED POEMS,

And private

EJACULATIONS.

BY

Mr. *George Herbert*,

· late ORATOUR of the
Univerfity of
CAMBRIDGE.

*The Eighth Edition, with an Alphabeticall
Table for ready finding out chief places.*

PSAL. 29.
In his Temple doth every man fpeak of his honour.

LONDON,
Printed by *R. N.* for *Philemon Stephens,*
at the Gilded Lyon in S. *Pauls Church-yard*
1 6 6 o.

THE
ΓEMPLE.
SACRED POEMS,
And Private
EJACULATIONS.

BY
Mr *George Herbert*,
Late ORATOUR of the
Univerfity of
CAMBRIDGE.

The Ninth Edition, with an *Alphabetical*
Ta ble for ready finding out chief places.

PSAL. 29.
In his Temple doth every man fpeak of his honour.

LONDON,
Printed by *J. M.* for *Philemon Stephens*,
and are to be Sold at the *Kings Arms*
in *Chancery*-Lane, 1 6 6 7.

THE
TEMPLE.
SACRED POEMS,
And Private
EJACULATIONS.

BY
Mr. *George Herbert*
Late ORATOUR of the
Univerſity of
CAMBRIDGE.

*The Ninth Edition, with an Alphabetical
Table for ready finding out chief places.*

PSAL. 29.
In his Temple doth every man ſpeak of his honour.

LONDON,
Printed by *J.M.* for *Philemon Stephens,*
at the *Kings-Arms* in *Chancery-Lane,*
and *J.Stephens* at the *Black-Prince*
in *Duck-Lane.* 1667.

THE
TEMPLE.

SACRED POEMS
AND PRIVATE
EJACULATIONS.

By Mr *George Herbert*,
Late ORATOUR of the
Univerſity of *CAMBRIDGE*.

Together with his L I F E. *with
ſeveral Additions.*

PSAL. 29.
In his Temple doth every man ſpeak of his honour.

*The Tenth Edition, with an Alphabetical
Table for ready finding out the chief places.*

LONDON,
Printed by *W. Godbid*, for *R. S.* and are to
be Sold by *John Williams* Junior, in *Croſs-
Key* Court in *Little-Britain*, 1674.

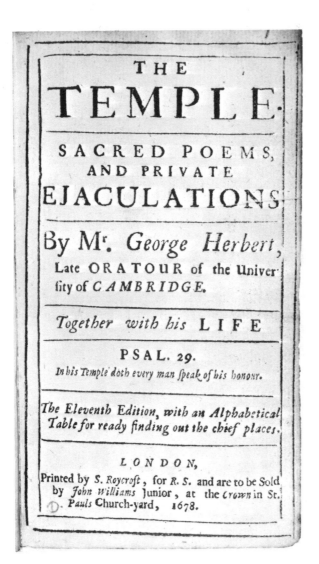

THE
TEMPLE.

SACRED POEMS,
AND PRIVATE
EJACULATIONS

By Mr. *George Herbert*,
Late ORATOUR of the Univerfity of *CAMBRIDGE.*

Together with his LIFE

PSAL. 29.
In his Temple doth every man speak of his honour.

*The Eleventh Edition, with an Alphabetical
Table for ready finding out the chief places.*

LONDON,
Printed by S. *Roycroft*, for *R. S.* and are to be Sold
by *John Williams* Junior, at the *Crown* in St.
(D. *Pauls* Church-yard, 1678.

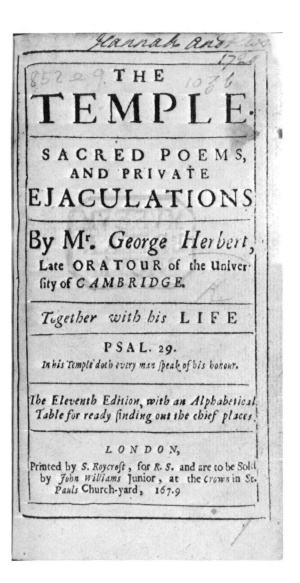

THE

TEMPLE.

SACRED POEMS,
AND PRIVATE

EJACULATIONS

By M*r*. *George Herbert,*
Late ORATOUR of the University of *CAMBRIDGE.*

Together with his LIFE

PSAL. 29.
In his Temple doth every man speak of his honour.

The Eleventh Edition, with an Alphabetical Table for ready finding out the chief places.

LONDON,
Printed by *S. Roycroft*, for *R. S.* and are to be Sold by *John Williams* Junior, at the *Crown* in St. *Pauls* Church-yard, 1679.

HERBERT.   PLATE 24 (No. 18a).   B.M.(852.e.9).

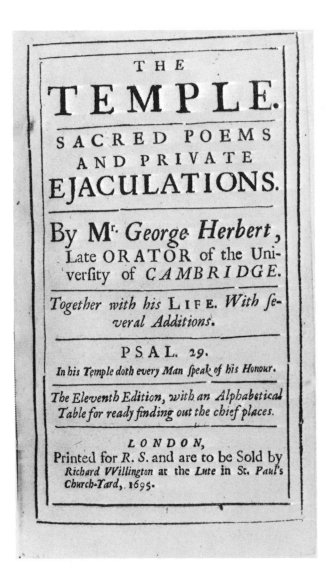

THE

TEMPLE.

SACRED POEMS
AND PRIVATE
EJACULATIONS.

By Mr. *George Herbert*,
Late ORATOR of the Uni-
verſity of *CAMBRIDGE*.

Together with his LIFE. *With ſe-*
veral Additions.

PSAL. 29.
In his Temple doth every Man ſpeak of his Honour.

The Eleventh Edition, with an Alphabetical
Table for ready finding out the chief places.

LONDON,
Printed for *R. S.* and are to be Sold by
Richard Willington at the *Lute* in St. *Paul's*
Church-Yard, 1695.

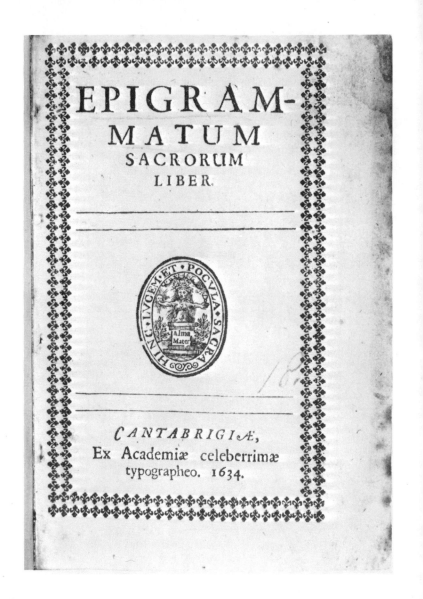

EPIGRAM-
MATUM
SACRORUM
LIBER.

CANTABRIGIÆ,
Ex Academiæ celeberrimæ
typographeo. 1634.

CRASHAW. PLATE 1 (No. 1).   Bodl. (8°.E.76.Th).

Richardi Crashawi

POEMATA
ET
EPIGRAMMATA,
Quæ fcripfit Latina & Græca,

Dum *Aulæ Pemb.* Alumnus fuit,
Et
Collegii *Petrenfis* Socius.

Editio Secunda, Auctior & emendatior.

Εἵνεκεν ευμαθίης πινυτόφρον☉, ἥν ὁ Μελιχρὸς
Ἤσκησεν, Μεσῶν ἄμμιγα κỳ Χαείπων.   Ἀνθολ.

CANTABRIGIÆ,
ix Officina *Joan. Hayes*, Celeberrimæ Academiæ
Typographi. 1670.

CRASHAW.   PLATE 2 (No. 2).   Bodl.(Douce.cc.29/1).

Richardi Crashawi

POEMATA
ET
EPIGRAMMATA,
Quæ fcripfit Latina & Græca,
Dum *Aulæ Pemb.* Alumnus fuit,
Et
Collegii *Petrenfis* Socius.

Editio Secunda, Auctior & emendatior.

Εἵνεκεν ευμαϑἰης πινυτώτεϼνοι, ἧν ὁ Μελιχϼὸς
ᾟσκησεν, Μυσῶν ἀμμιγα χαὶ Χαεἰτων.   Ἀνϑολ.

CANTABRIGIÆ,

Ex Officina *Joan. Hayes,* Celeberrimæ Academiæ
Typographi. 1674.
Proftant Venales apud *Joann. Creed.*

CRASHAW.   PLATE 3 (No. 3).   Bodl.(Vet.A3.f.818).

Richardi Crashawi

POEMATA
ET
EPIGRAMMATA,

Quæ ſcripſit Latina & Græca,
Dum *Aulæ Pemb.* Alumnus fuit,
Et
Collegii *Petrenſis* Socius.

Editio Secunda, Auctior & emendatior.

Εἴϱεϰεν ἐυμαϑίης ϖινυτίφϱϱνος, ἤν ὁ Μελιχϱϱς
Ἡσϰησϖν, Μϱσϖν ἄμμιγα ϰϱι Χαείτων. 'Ανϑολ.

1ᵒ *CANTABRIGIÆ,*
Ex Officina *Joan.* Hayes, Celeberrimæ Academiæ
Typographi. 1674.
Proſtant Venales apud *Joann.* Creed.

EPIGRAMMATA

Sacra Selecta,

CUM

ANGLICA VERSIONE.

SACRED
EPIGRAMS
Englished.

LONDON,

Printed for *John Barksdale*, Book-seller
in *Cirencester*, 1682.

CRASHAW.   PLATE 5 (No. 4).   Bodl.(Vet.a3.f.270/2).

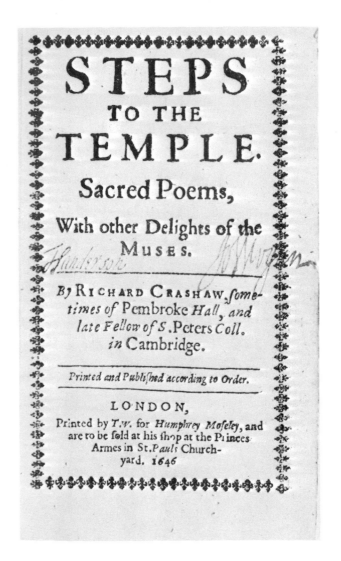

STEPS
TO THE
TEMPLE.
Sacred Poems,

With other Delights of the
MUSES.

By RICHARD CRASHAW, *sometimes of* Pembroke Hall, *and late Fellow of* S.Peters Coll. *in* Cambridge.

Printed and Published according to Order.

LONDON,

Printed by *T.w.* for *Humphrey Moseley*, and are to be sold at his shop at the Princes Armes in St.*Pauls* Church-yard. 1646

CRASHAW. PLATE 6 (No. 5). B.M.(E.220/2).

91

A LETTER

FROM

M.r CRASHAW

to the

Countess of DENBIGH,

Against Irresolution and Delay in matters of RELIGION.

Sept: 23

LONDON.
1653

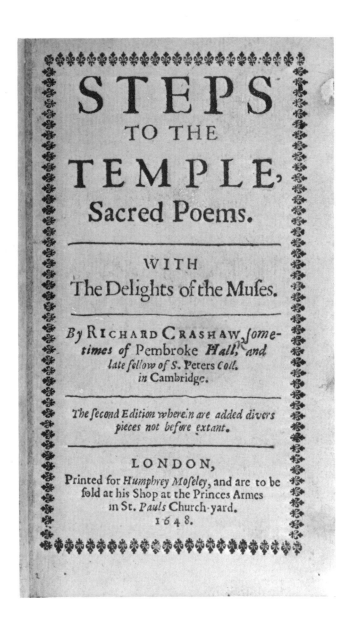

STEPS

TO THE

TEMPLE,

Sacred Poems.

WITH

The Delights of the Muses.

By RICHARD CRASHAW, *sometimes of* Pembroke *Hall, and late fellow of* S. *Peters Coll. in* Cambridge.

The second Edition wherein are added divers pieces not before extant.

LONDON,

Printed for *Humphrey Moseley*, and are to be sold at his Shop at the Princes Armes in St. *Pauls* Church-yard.
1 6 4 8.

CARMEN
DEO NOSTRO,
TE DECET HYMNVS
SACRED POEMS,
COLLECTED,
CORRECTED,
AVGMENTED,
Moſt humbly Preſented;

TO

MY LADY
THE COVNTSSE OF
DENBIGH
BY

Her moſt deuoted Seruant;

R. C.

In heaty acknowledgment of his immortall
obligation to her Goodnes & Charity.

Wimu but now ego to Land

9 September 1655

AT PARIS,

By PETER TARGA, Printer to the Arch-
biſhope ef Paris, in S. Victors ſtreete at
the golden ſunne.

M. DC. LII.

·STEPS

TO THE

TEMPLE,

THE

DELIGHTS

OF THE

MUSE'S,

AND

CARMEN

DEO NOSTRO·

By *Ric. Crashaw*, sometimes Fellow of *Pembroke Hall*, and late Fellow of *St Peters Colledge* in *Cambridge.*

The 2d *Edition.*

In the *SAVOY*,

Printed by *T. N.* for *Henry Herringman* at the *Blew Anchor* in the *Lower Walk* of the *New Exchange.* 1670.

STEPS
TO THE
TEMPLE,
THE
DELIGHTS
OF THE
MUSES,
AND
CARMEN
DEO NOSTRO.

By *Ric. Crashaw*, fometimes Fellow of *Pembroek Hall*, and Fellow of *St. Peters Colledge* in *Cambridge*.

The Third Edition.

LONDON,
Printed for *Richard Bently*. *Jacob Tonson*,
Francis Saunders, and *Th. Bennet*.

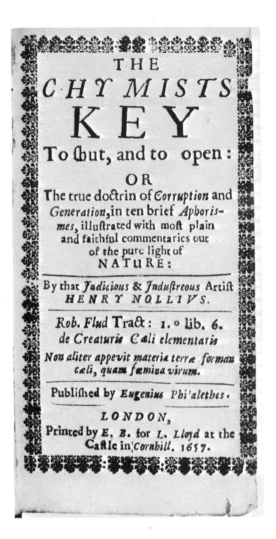

THE
CHYMISTS
KEY

To ſhut, and to open:

OR

The true doctrin of *Corruption* and
Generation, in ten brief *Aphoris-
mes*, illuſtrated with moſt plain
and faithful commentaries out
of the pure light of
NATURE:

By that *Judicious* & *Industreous* Artiſt
HENRY NOLLIVS.

Rob. Flud Tract: 1. ° lib. 6.
de Creaturis Cœli elementaris
*Non aliter appevit materia terræ formam
cœli, quam fœmina virum.*

Publiſhed by *Eugenius* *Phi'alethes.*

LONDON,
Printed by *E, B.* for *L. Lloyd* at the
Caſtle in *Cornbill.* 1657.

Flores Solitudinis.
Certaine Rare and Elegant
PIECES;
Viz.

Two Excellent Difcourfes
Of $\left\{\begin{array}{l}\text{1. Temperance, and Patience;} \\ \text{2. Life and Death.}\end{array}\right.$
BY
I. E. NIEREMBERGIUS.

THE WORLD
CONTEMNED;
BY
EUCHERIUS, BP of LYONS.

And the Life of
PAULINUS,
BP of *NOLA.*

Collected in his Sickneffe and Retirement
BY
HENRY VAUGHAN, Silurift.

Tantus Amor Florum, & generandi gloria Mellis.

London, Printed for *Humphrey Mofeley* at the
Princes Armes in St *Pauls* Church-yard. 1654.

HERMETICAL
PHYSICK:
O R,
The right way to pre-
ferve, and to reftore
HEALTH.

B Y
That famous and faith-
full Chymift,

HENRY NOLLIVS.

Englifhed by
HENRY UAUGHAN, Gent.

LONDON.
Printed for *Humphrey Mofeley,* and
are to be fold at his fhop, at the
Princes Armes in St. *Pauls Church-
Yard,* 1 6 5 5.

VAUGHAN. PLATE 3 (No. 3).   B.M.(E.1714/1).

THE MOUNT of OLIVES:

OR,

SOLITARY DEVOTIONS.

By

HENRY VAVGHAN *Silurist.*

With

An excellent Difcourfe of the bleffed ftate of MAN in GLORY, written by the moft Reverend and holy Father ANSELM Arch-Bifhop of *Canterbury,* and now done into Englifh.

LUKE 2r. v. 39, 37.

Watch ye therefore, and pray always, that ye may be accompted worthy to efcape all thefe things that fhall come to paffe, and to ftand before the Sonne of Man.
And in the day time he was teaching in the Temple, and at night he went out, and abode in the Mount that is called the Mount of Olives.

LONDON, Printed for WILLIAM LEAKE at the Crown in Fleet-ftreet between the two Temple-Gates. 1 6 5 2

OLOR ISCANUS. ✗

A COLLECTION

OF SOME SELECT

POEMS,

AND

TRANSLATIONS,

Formerly written by

*Mr.*Henry Vaugħan *Siluriſt.*

Publiſhed by a Friend.

V*i*g. Georg.
Flumina amo, Sylvaſq, Inglorius———

LONDON,

Printed by *T.W.* for *Humphreÿ Moſeley,*
and are to be ſold at his ſhop, at the
Signe of the Prince's Arms in St.*Pauls*
Church-yard, 1651.

OLOR ISCANVS.

A COLLECTION

Of some SELECT

POEMS,

Together with thefe Tranflations following, *viz.*

1. Of the benefit wee may get by our *Enemies,*

2. Of the difeafes of the mind, and of the body. Both
written in *Greek,* by that great *Philofopher Plutarch.*

3. Of the difeafes of the mind, and of the body, and
which of them is moft pernicious, written in *Greek* by
Maximus Tyrius.

4. Of the praife and happinefs of a Country Life ;
written in *Spanifh* by *Antonio de Guevara :* Bifhop of
Carthagena.

All Englifhed by *H. Vaughan, Silurift.*

LONDON:

Printed, and are to be fold by *Peter Parker,*
at the *Leg* and *Star* in *Cornhil,* againft the
Royal Exchange, 1679.

VAUGHAN.   PLATE 6 (No. 6).   N.L.W.

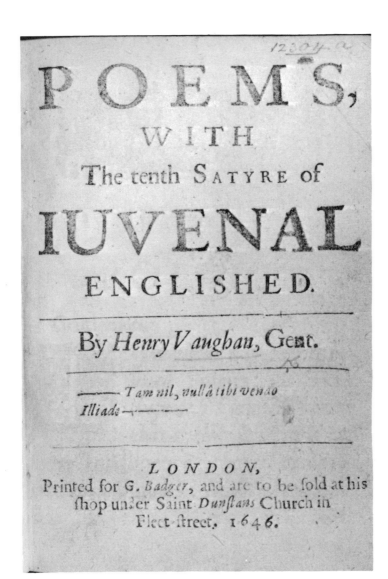

POEMS,

WITH

The tenth SATYRE of

IUVENAL

ENGLISHED.

By *Henry Vaughan,* Gent.

——— *Tam nil, nullâ tibi vendo*
Illiade—————

LONDON,
Printed for G. *Badger,* and are to be sold at his
shop under Saint *Dunstans* Church in
Fleet-street. 1646.

Silex Scintillans:
or
SACRED POEMS
and
Priuate Eiaculations
By
Henry Vaughan Silurist

LONDON Printed by T.W. for H. Blunden
at y Castle in Cornehill. 1650

VAUGHAN. PLATE 8 (No. 8). B.M. (238.b.8).

Silex Scintillans:

SACRED

POEMS

And private

EJACULATIONS.

The second Edition, In two Books;
By *Henry Vaughan*, Silurist.

Job chap 35 ver. 10, 11.

Where is God my Maker, who giveth Songs in
the night?
Who teacheth us more then the beasts of the
earth, and maketh us wiser then the fowls
of heaven?

London, Printed for *Henry Crips*, and *Lodo-*
wick Lloyd, next to the Castle in *Cornhil*,
and in *Popes-head Alley*. 1655.

Thalia Rediviva:

THE
Pass-Times and Diversions
OF A
COUNTREY-MUSE,

In Choice

POEMS

On several Occasions.

By mr Henry Vaughan the Silurist.

WITH

Some Learned *Remains* of the Eminent

Eugenius Philalethes.

Never made Publick till now.

———Nec erubuit sylvas habitare Thalia. *Virgil.*

Licensed, *Roger L'Estrange.*

London, Printed for *Robert Pawlet* at the Bible in
Chancery-lane, near *Fleetstreet,* 1 6 7 8.

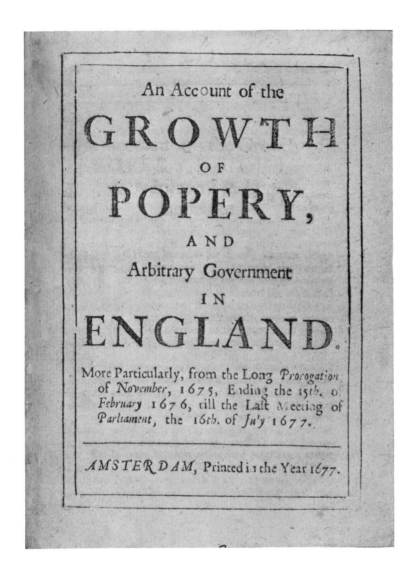

An Account of the

GROWTH

OF

POPERY,

AND

Arbitrary Government

IN

ENGLAND.

More Particularly, from the Long *Prorogation* of *November*, 1675, Ending the 15*th*, of *February* 1676, till the Laſt Meeting of *Parliament*, the 16*th*. of *Ju'y* 1677.

AMSTERDAM, Printed in the Year 1677.

MARVELL.　PLATE 1 (No. 1).　　　　　B.M.(Ashley 1104).

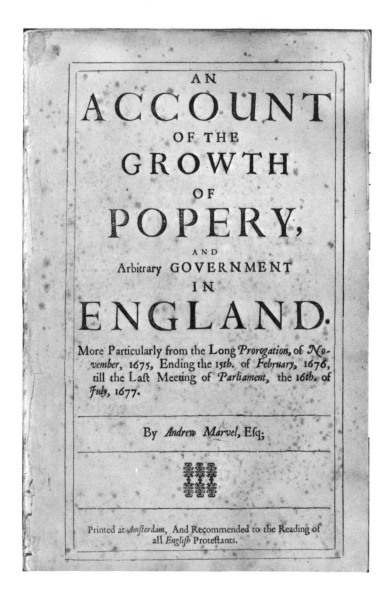

AN
ACCOUNT
OF THE
GROWTH
OF
POPERY,
AND
Arbitrary GOVERNMENT
IN
ENGLAND.

More Particularly from the Long *Prorogation*, of *No-vember*, 1675, Ending the 15th. of *February*, 1676, till the Laft Meeting of *Parliament*, the 16th. of *July*, 1677.

By *Andrew Marvel*, Efq;

Printed at *Amfterdam*, And Recommended to the Reading of all *Englifh* Proteftants.

MARVELL.   PLATE 2 (No. 2).   B.M.(4707.h.12).

RELATION

D E

l'Accroiſſement de la

PAPAUTÉ

Et du Gouvernement Abſolu en

ANGLETERRE,

Particulierement

Depuis la longue Prorogation de
Novembre 1675. laquelle a fini
le 15. Fevrier 1676.
juſques à preſent.

Traduit en François de la Copie Angloiſe.

A HAMBOURGH,
Chez *Pierre Pladt*, Libraire, 1680.

𝕸𝖗. 𝕬𝖓𝖉𝖗𝖊𝖜 𝕸𝖆𝖗𝖛𝖊𝖑𝖑'𝖘

CHARACTER .

OF

POPERY.

January 17. 168⅞. This may be Printed.

ROB. MIDGLEY.

L O N D O N,
Printed for *R I C H A R D B A L D W I N,*
next the *Black Bull,* in the *Old-Bailey.*
M DC LXXX IX.

THE

CHARACTER

OF

HOLLAND.

*H*olland, that fcarce deferves the name
of Land,
As but th' Of-fcowring of the *Brit-
tifh* Sand ;
And fo much Earth as was contributed
By *Englifh* Pilots, when they heav'd the Lead ;
Or what by th' Oceans flow alluvion fell
Of Shipwrackt Cockle and the Mufle fhell ;
This Indigefted Vomit of the Sea
Fell to the *Dutch* by juft Proprietie.

A Glad

7

Vainly did this *Slap-Dragon* fury hope,

With fober *Englifh* valour ere to cope:

Not though they Primed their barbarous mor-
nings-draught

With Powder, and with Pipes of Brandy fraught:

Yet *Rupert, Sandwich,* and of all, the *Duke,*

The *Duke* has made their Sea-fick courage puke.

Like the three Comets, fent from heaven down

With Fiery Flailes to fwinge th' ingratefull
Clown.

FINIS.

London, *Printed by* T. Mabb *for* Robert Horn
at the Angel *in* Popes-head alley, 1665.

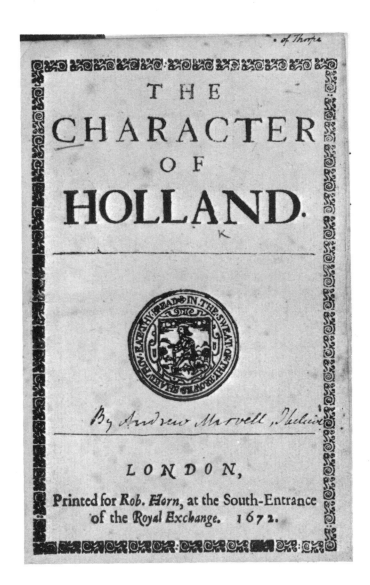

THE
CHARACTER
OF
HOLLAND.

By *Andrew Marvell*, *Theliie*

LONDON,

Printed for *Rob. Horn,* at the South-Entrance
of the *Royal Exchange.* 1672.

MARVELL.   PLATE 7 (No. 6).   B.M.(C.71.h.13).

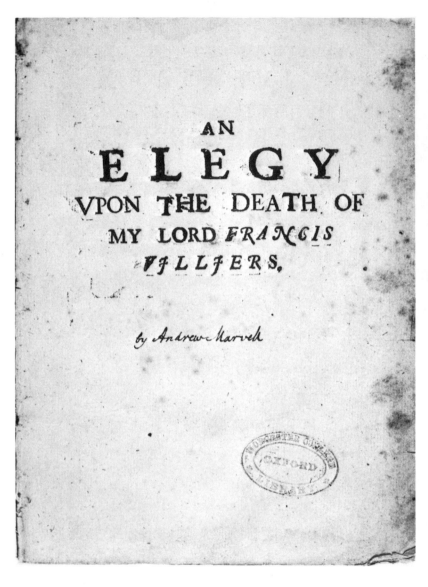

AN
ELEGY
VPON THE DEATH OF
MY LORD *FRANCIS*
VILLIERS,

by Andrew Marvell

THE *FIRST*

ANNIVERSARY

OF THE

GOVERNMENT

UNDER

HIS HIGHNESS

THE

Lord Protector.

LONDON,

Printed by *Thomas Newcomb*, and are to be fold by
Samuel Gellibrand at the golden Ball in *Pauls*
Church-yard, near the Weft end,
Anno. Dom: 1 6 5 5.

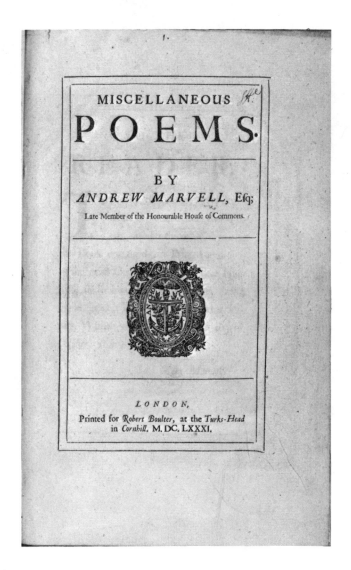

MISCELLANEOUS

POEMS.

BY
ANDREW MARVELL, Eſq;
Late Member of the Honourable Houſe of Commons.

LONDON,
Printed for *Robert Boulter*, at the *Turks-Head*
in *Cornhill.* M. DC. LXXXI.

MARVELL. PLATE 10 (No. 9) (Greatly reduced). B.M.(C.59.i8).

8

Mr. SMIRKE:

OR, THE

3

DIVINE in MODE:

BEING

Certain *Annotations*, upon the *Animadversions* on the *Naked Truth*.

Together with a Short *Historical Essay*,
concerning *General Councils*, *Creeds*, and *Impositions*, in Matters of *Religion*.

Nuda, sed Magna est Veritas, & prævalebit.

B Y

ANDREAS RIVETUS, *Junior.*

Anagr.

RES NUDA VERITAS.

Printed *Anno Domini* M DC LXXVI.

MARVELL.   PLATE II (No. 10).   Trinity College, Dublin (P.gg.21/3).

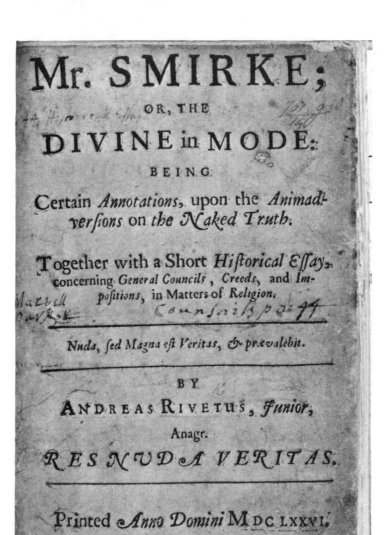

Mr. SMIRKE;

OR, THE

DIVINE in MODE:

BEING

Certain *Annotations*, upon the *Animad-*
verfions on *the Naked Truth.*

Together with a Short *Hiftorical Effay*,
concerning *General Councils* , *Creeds*, and *Im-*
pofitions, in Matters of *Religion.*

Nuda, fed Magna eft Veritas, & prævalebit.

BY

ANDREAS RIVETUS, *Junior*,

Anagr.

RES NVDA VERITAS.

Printed *Anno Domini* M DC LXXVI.

more

MARVELL. PLATE 12 (No. 10a). B.M.(701.g.10/14).

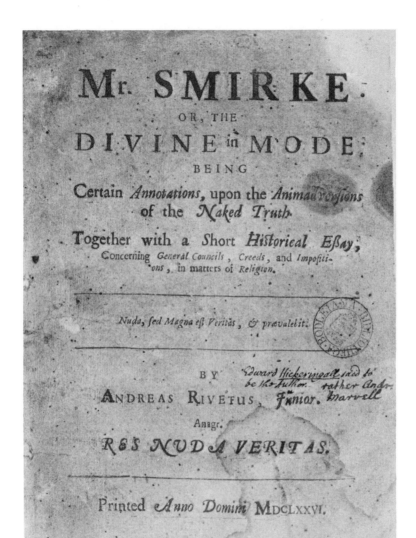

Mr. SMIRKE:

OR, THE

DIVINE in MODE:

BEING

Certain *Annotations*, upon the *Animadversions*
of the *Naked Truth.*

Together with a Short *Historical Essay,*
Concerning *General Councils*, *Creeds*, and *Impositi-*
ons, in matters of *Religion.*

Nuda, sed Magna est Veritas, & prævalebit.

BY

ANDREAS RIVETUS, *Junior.*

Anagr.

RES NUDA VERITAS.

Printed *Anno Domini* MDCLXXVI.

MARVELL. PLATE 13 (No. 11).   Bodl. (D.12.1 Linc/4).

119

THE
REHEARSAL
TRANSPROS'D:
Or,
Animadversions
Upon a late Book, Intituled,
A PREFACE
SHEWING
What Grounds there are of Fears and Jealousies of Popery.

LONDON, Printed by *A.B.* for the Assigns of *John Calvin* and *Theodore Beza*, at the sign of the Kings Indulgence, on the South-side of the *Lake Lemane*. 1672.

THE
REHEARSAL
TRANSPROS'D:

Or,

Animadverfions

Upon a late Book, Intituled,

A PREFACE
SHEWING

*What Grounds there are
of Fears and Jealoufies
of* Popery.

LONDON

Printed in the Year, 1 6 7 2.

$\mathcal{R}\ \mathcal{W}\ \mathcal{P}.$ THE

REHEARSAL
TRANSPROS'D:
OR,

Animadverfions

Upon a late BOOK, entituled,

A PREFACE,
SHEWING

What Grounds there are
of Fears and Jealoufies
of Popery.

LONDON,
Printed in the Year, **1672.**

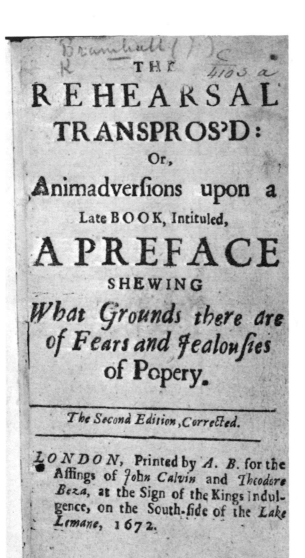

THE
REHEARSAL
TRANSPROS'D:
Or,
Animadversions upon a
Late BOOK, Intituled,
A PREFACE
SHEWING
What Grounds there are of Fears and Jealousies of Popery.

The Second Edition, Corrected.

LONDON, Printed by *A. B.* for the
Affings of *John Calvin* and *Theodore
Beza*, at the Sign of the Kings Indul-
gence, on the South-fide of the *Lake
Lemane,* 1672.

THE
REHEARSAL
TRANSPROS'D;
Or,
Animadversions
Upon a late Book, Intituled,

A PREFACE
SHEWING
What Grounds there are
of Fears and Jealousies
of Popery.

The second Impression, with Additions
and Amendments.

London, Printed by *J. D.* for the Assigns of
John Calvin and *Theodore Beza*, at the sign
of the *King's Indulgence*, on the South-side
the Lake-*Lemane*; and sold by *N. Ponder* in
Chancery-Lane, 1672.

THE
REHEARSAL
TRANSPROS'D;
O R,

Animadversions

Upon a late BOOK,

INTITULED,

A PREFACE, *shewing what Grounds there are of Fears and Jealousies of Popery.*

The second Impression, with Additions and Amendments.

LONDON, Printed by *J. D.* for the Assigns of *John Calvin* and *Theodore Beza* at the sign of the *King's Indulgence* on the South-side of the *Lake Lemane*; and Sould by *N. Ponder* in *Chancery Lane*, 1672.

THE
REHEARSAL
TRANSPROS'D;

OR,

ANIMADVERSIONS

Upon a late Book, Intituled, A

PREFACE

SHEWING

What Grounds there are of Fears and Jealousies of *Popery*.

The second Impression, with Additions and Amendments.

London, Printed by *J. X.* for the Assigns of *John Calvin* and *Theodore Beza* , at the sign of the *King's Indulgence*; on the South-side the Lake-*Leman*. 1673.

THE
REHEARSALL
TRANSPROS'D:

The SECOND PART.

Occasioned by Two Letters : The first.
Printed , by a namelefs Author,
Intituled, A Reproof, &c.
The Second Letter left for me at a
Friends Houfe , Dated Nov. 3.
1 6 7 3. Subfcribed J. G. *and*
concluding with thefe words ; If
thou dareft to Print or Publifh
any Lie or Libel againft Doctor
Parker , By the Eternal God I
will cut thy Throat.

Anfwered by ANDREW MARVEL

LONDON,
Printed for Nathaniel Ponder *at the* Peacock *in*
Chancery Lane *near* Fleet-Street, 1673.

THE
REHEARSALL
TRANSPROSD:

The SECOND PART.

Occafioned by Two Letters : The firft Print-ed, by a namelefs Author, Intituled A Reproof, *&c.*

The Second Letter left for me at a Friends Houfe, Dated Nov. 3. 1 6 7 3. Subfcri-bed J. G. *and concluding with thefe words,* If thou dareft to Print or Publifh any Lie or Libel againft Doctor *Parker,* By the Eternal God I will cut thy Throat.

Anfwered by ANDREW MARVEL

L O N D O N,
Printed for Nathaniel Ponder *at the* Peacock *in* Chancery-Lane *near* Fleet-Street, 1 6 7 4.

MARVELL.   PLATE 22 (No. 17).   B.M.(1607/3406).

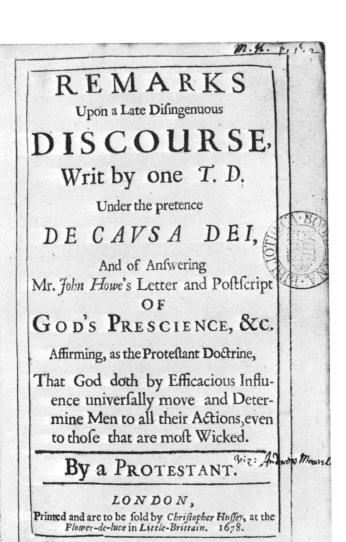

REMARKS

Upon a Late Disingenuous

DISCOURSE,

Writ by one *T. D.*

Under the pretence

DE CAVSA DEI,

And of Answering

Mr. *John Howe's* Letter and Postscript

OF

GOD'S PRESCIENCE, &c.

Affirming, as the Protestant Doctrine,

That God doth by Efficacious Influence universally move and Determine Men to all their Actions, even to those that are most Wicked.

By a PROTESTANT.

LONDON,

Printed and are to be sold by *Christopher Hussey*, at the *Flower-de-luce* in *Little-Brittain.* 1678.

A SHORT
HISTORICAL
ESSAY
TOUCHING

GENERAL COUNCILS,
CREEDS, and
IMPOSITIONS in Matters of Religion.

Very Seasonable for Allaying the Heats of the

CHURCH.

Written by that Ingenious and Worthy Gentleman
Mr. ANDREW MARVELL,
Who died a Member of Parliament.

LONDON:
Printed in the Year MDCLXXX.

A SHORT

HISTORICAL

ESSAY

TOUCHING

GENERAL COUNCILS,

CREEDS, *and*

IMPOSITIONS *in Matters of Religion.*

Very Seafonable at this Time.

Written by

ANDREW MARVEL, Efq;

LONDON,
Printed for *R. Baldwin,* 1687.

B., E. Vaughan 1.
Badger, George. Vaughan 7.
Baldwin, Richard. Marvell 4, 20.
Barksdale, John. Crashaw 4.
Bennet, Thomas. Crashaw 10.
Bently, Richard. Crashaw 10.
Blunden, Humphrey. Herbert 2, Vaughan 8.
Boulter, Robert. Marvell 9.
Brewster, Anne. Marvell 12.
Buck, Thomas. Herbert 7, 7a, 8, 8a, 9, 10, 11.
Cambridge, University Press. Crashaw 1.
Creed, John. Crashaw 2, 3.
Crips, Henry. Vaughan 9.
Daniel, Roger. Herbert 7, 7a, 8, 8a, 9, 10, 11, 12.
Darby, John. Marvell 14.
Garthwait, Timothy. Herbert 3, 6.
Gellibrand, Samuel. Marvell 8.
Godbid, William. Herbert 17.
Green, Francis. Herbert 8a, 9.
Hayes, John. Crashaw 2, 3.
Herringman, Henry. Crashaw 9.
Horn, Robert. Marvell 5, 6.
Hussey, Christopher. Marvell 18.
Leake, William. Vaughan 4.
Legatt, John. Herbert 13.
Legge, Cantrell. Herbert 1.
Lloyd, Lodowick. Vaughan 1, 9.
M., J. Herbert 16, 16a.
Mabb, Thomas. Marvell 5.
Maxey, Thomas. Herbert 3, 6.
Moseley, Humphrey. Crashaw 6, 7, Vaughan 2, 3, 5.
N., T. Crashaw 9.
Newcomb, Thomas. Marvell 8.
Norton, Roger. Herbert 15.
Paine, Thomas. Herbert 2.
Parker, Peter. Vaughan 6.
Pawlet, Robert. Vaughan 10.
Pladt, Pierre. Marvell 3.
Ponder, Nathaniel. Marvell 12, 14, 16, 17.
Roycroft, Samuel. Herbert 18.
Roycroft, Thomas. Herbert 4, 5, 14.
Saunders, Francis. Crashaw 10.
Stephens, John. Herbert 16a.
Stephens, Philemon. Herbert 13, 14, 15, 16, 16a.
Stephens, Robert. Herbert 17, 18, 19.
Targa, Peter. Crashaw 8.

Tonson, Jacob. Crashaw 10.
Tooke, Benjamin. Herbert 4, 5.
W., T. Crashaw 6, Vaughan 5, 8.
Williams, John, *junior.* Herbert 17, 18.
Willington, Richard. Herbert 19.
X., J. Marvell 15.